Quest

Second Edition

1

 **Reading and Writing**

Pamela Hartmann
Laurie Blass

 **McGraw-Hill**

Quest 1 Reading and Writing, 2nd Edition

ISBN 13: 978-0-07-353390-2
ISBN 10: 0-07-353390-4
1 2 3 4 5 6 7 8 9 VNH/VNH 12 11 10 09 08 07 06

ISBN 13: 978-0-07-110334-3 (International Student Book)
ISBN 10: 0-07-110334-1
1 2 3 4 5 6 7 8 9 VNH/VNH 12 11 10 09 08 07 06

Editorial director: Erik Gundersen
Series editor: Linda O'Roke
Production editor: MaryRose Malley
Cover designer: David Averbach, Anthology
Interior designer: Martini Graphic Services, Inc.
Artists: Jonathan Massie, Ron Mahoney
Photo researcher: David Averbach, PoYee Oster

www.esl-elt.mcgraw-hill.com

The McGraw·Hill Companies

# ACKNOWLEDGEMENTS

The publisher and authors would like to thank the following education professionals whose comments, reviews, and assistance were instrumental in the development of the Quest series.

- **Roberta Alexander,** San Diego Community College District
- **David Dahnke,** North Harris College (Houston, TX)
- **Mary Díaz,** Broward Community College (Davie, FL)
- **Judith García,** Miami-Dade College
- **Elizabeth Giles,** The School District of Hillsborough County, Florida
- **Patricia Heiser,** University of Washington, Seattle
- **Yoshiko Matsubayashi,** Kokusai Junior College, Tokyo
- **Ahmed Motala,** University of Sharjah, United Arab Emirates
- **Dee Parker and Andy Harris,** AUA, Bangkok
- **Alison Rice,** Hunter College, City University of New York
- **Alice Savage,** North Harris College (Houston, TX)
- **Katharine Sherak,** San Francisco State University
- **Leslie Eloise Somers,** Miami-Dade County Public Schools
- **Karen Stanley,** Central Piedmont Community College (Charlotte, NC)
- **Diane Urairat,** Mahidol Language Services, Bangkok
- **Pamela Vittorio,** The New School (New York, NY)
- **Anne Marie Walters,** California State University, Long Beach
- **Lynne Wilkins,** Mills College (Oakland, CA)
- **Sean Wray, Elizabeth Watson, and Mariko Yokota,** Waseda International University, Tokyo

Many, many thanks go to Marguerite Ann Snow, who provided the initial inspiration for the entire series. Heartfelt thanks also to Erik Gundersen and Linda O'Roke for their help in the development of the second edition. We'd also like to thank Dylan Bryan-Dolman, Susannah MacKay, Kristin Sherman, and Kristin Thalheimer, whose opinions were invaluable.

TABLE OF CONTENTS

Quest: The Series

Quest Second Edition prepares students for academic success. The series features two complementary strands—*Reading and Writing* and *Listening and Speaking*—each with four levels. The integrated Quest program provides robust scaffolding to support and accelerate each student's journey from exploring general interest topics to mastering academic content.

Quest parallels and accelerates the process native-speaking students go through when they prepare for success in a variety of academic subjects. By previewing typical college course material, *Quest* helps students get "up to speed" in terms of both academic content and language skills.

In addition, *Quest* prepares students for the daunting amount and type of reading, writing, listening, and speaking required for college success. The four *Reading and Writing* books combine high-interest material from newspapers and magazines with readings from academic textbooks. Reading passages increase in length and difficulty across the four levels. The *Listening and Speaking* books in the *Quest* series contain listening strategies and practice activities based on authentic audio and video recordings from "person on the street" interviews, radio programs, and college lectures. Similar to the *Reading and Writing* books, the four *Listening and Speaking* books increase in difficulty with each level.

Quest Second Edition Features

- New *Intro* level providing on-ramp to Books 1-3
- Redesigned, larger format with captivating photos
- Expanded focus on critical thinking and test-taking strategies
- Addition of research paper to *Reading and Writing* strand
- New unit-ending *Vocabulary Workshops* and end-of-book academic word lists
- Expanded video program (VHS and DVD) with new lecture and updated social language footage
- EZ Test® CD-ROM-based test generator for all *Reading and Writing* titles
- Teacher's Editions with activity-by-activity procedural notes, expansion activities, and tests
- Test-taking strategy boxes that highlight skills needed for success on the new TOEFL® iBT test

Quest Reading and Writing

Quest Reading and Writing includes three or four distinct units, each focusing on a different area of college study—sociology, biology, business, history, psychology, art history, anthropology, literature, or economics. Each unit contains two thematically-related chapters.

TOEFL is a registered trademark of Educational Testing Service (ETS). This publication is not endorsed or approved by ETS.

Chapter Structure

Each chapter of *Quest Intro Reading and Writing* contains five parts that blend reading and writing skills within the context of a particular academic area of study. Readings and activities build upon one another and increase in difficulty as students work through the five sections of each chapter.

Part 1: Introduction
- Before Reading – discussion activities on photos introduce the chapter topic
- Reading – a high-interest reading captures students' attention
- After Reading – activities check students' understanding and allow for further discussion

Part 2: General Interest Reading
- Before Reading – prediction and vocabulary activities prepare students for reading
- Reading – a high-interest reading at a slightly higher level than the reading in Part 1 allows students to explore the chapter topic in more depth
- After Reading – comprehension, discussion, and vocabulary activities check understanding

Part 3: Academic Reading
- Before Reading – prediction and vocabulary activities prepare students for reading
- Reading – a textbook selection prepares students for academic reading
- After Reading – strategies (such as skimming for main ideas, using a dictionary, and synthesizing) and activities give students the opportunity to use academic skills

Part 4: The Mechanics of Writing
- Chapter-specific writing, grammar, lexical, and punctuation boxes equip students to express their ideas.
- Content-driven grammar boxes are followed by contextualized practice activities that prepare students for independent writing assignments.

Part 5: Academic Writing
- A step-by-step model leads students through the writing process which may include brainstorming, narrowing the topic, writing topic sentences, planning the writing, and developing ideas into a paragraph.
- Writing assignments focus on a variety of rhetorical styles: chronological, description, analysis, persuasive, and process.
- Writing assignments ask students to use the writing mechanics taught.

Teacher's Editions

The *Quest Teacher's Editions* provide instructors with activity-by-activity teaching suggestions, cultural and background notes, Internet links to more information on the unit themes, expansion black-line master activities, chapter tests, and a complete answer key.

The *Quest Teacher's Editions* also provide test-taking boxes that highlight skills found in *Quest* that are needed for success on the new TOEFL® iBT test.

Video Program

For the *Quest Listening and Speaking* books, a newly expanded video program on DVD or VHS incorporates authentic classroom lectures with social language vignettes.

Lectures

The lecture portion of each video features college and university professors delivering high-interest mini-lectures on topics as diverse as animal communication, personal finance, and Greek art. The mini-lectures run from two minutes at the *Intro* level to six minutes by Book 3. As students listen to the lectures they complete structured outlines to model accurate note taking. Well-organized post-listening activities teach students how to use and refer to their notes in order to answer questions about the lecture and to review for a test.

Social Language

The social language portion of the videos gives students the chance to hear authentic conversations on topics relevant to the chapter topic and academic life. A series of scenes shot on or around an urban college campus features nine engaging students participating in a host of curricular and extracurricular activities. The social language portion of the video is designed to help English language students join study groups, interact with professors, and make friends.

Audio Program

Each reading selection on the audio CD or audiocassette program allows students to hear new vocabulary words, listen for intonation cues, and increase their reading speed. Each reading is recorded at an appropriate rate while remaining authentic.

Test Generator

For the *Quest Reading and Writing* books, an EZ Test® CD-ROM test generator allows teachers to create customized tests in a matter of minutes. EZ Test® is a flexible and easy-to-use desktop test generator. It allows teachers to create tests from unit-specific test banks or to write their own questions.

SCOPE AND SEQUENCE

Chapter	Reading Strategies	Writing Strategies
Getting Started • Introduction: *Getting the Most out of a Textbook*	• Guessing the Meaning from Context • Keeping a Word Journal • Understanding Parts of Speech • Understanding Parts of Speech: Suffixes • Using a Dictionary: Alphabetizing • Recognizing Main Ideas and Details • Recognizing Phrases and Clauses • Recognizing Topics and Main Ideas	• Choosing a Topic • Planning Your Paragraph • Writing the Paragraph • Editing • Rewriting
UNIT 1 BUSINESS		
Chapter 1 **Career Planning** • Introduction: *Cool Jobs* • General Interest: *Finding the Job That's Right for You* • Academic: *Your Major and Career: Myths and Possibilities*	• Guessing the Meanings of New Words: Definitions after *Be* or *Means*; Pictures and Captions • Recognizing Words in Phrases: Phrases with Prepositions • Connecting with the Topic	• Using a Graphic Organizer • Strategy: Determining the Main Idea • Focus: Paragraph Describing Your Ideal Job
Chapter 2 **The Free Enterprise System** • Introduction: *People in Business* • General Interest: *How the Market Works—Supply and Demand* • Academic: *Advertising*	• Guessing the Meanings of New Words: Commas, Dashes, Parentheses; *In Other Words* • Previewing: Having Questions in Mind • Using Topic Sentences	• Strategy: Organizing a Paragraph of Description • Focus: Paragraph Describing an Advertisement

The Mechanics of Writing	Critical Thinking Strategies	Test-Taking Strategies
• Parts of Speech • Parts of Speech: Suffixes	• Guessing the Meanings of New Words • Recognizing Main Ideas and Details • Recognizing Topics and Main Ideas	
UNIT 1 BUSINESS		
• Simple Present • Present Perfect • Time Expressions with the Present Perfect • Simple Past • Gerunds and Infinitives	• Applying Your Knowledge to New Situations • Using a Graphic Organizer	• Locating Key Words
• Prepositions of Place • Present Continuous • Stative Verbs • Using Adjectives • Using Multiple Adjectives	• Making Inferences • Previewing: Having Questions in Mind	• Finding Grammatical Errors

Chapter	Reading Strategies	Writing Strategies
UNIT 2 BIOLOGY		
Chapter 3: Animal Behavior • Introduction: *Animal Tales* • General Interest: *Animal Communication* • Academic: *How do Animals Learn?*	• Guessing the Meanings of New Words: *That Is*; *Such As* and *For Example* • Understanding Punctuation: Quotation Marks and Italics • Previewing for the Topic: Headings • Classifying	• Strategy: Organizing a Paragraph of Process • Focus: Paragraph Describing a Learned Behavior
Chapter 4: Nutrition • Introduction: *McDonald's Around the World* • General Interest: *Eating Bugs is Only Natural* • Academic: *Nutrition Basics*	• Guessing the Meanings of New Words: Using Examples • Understanding Italics • Previewing: Reading the Introduction • Previewing: Figures and Tables	• Strategy: Organizing a Paragraph of Analysis • Focus: Paragraph Analyzing a Diet
UNIT 3 U.S. HISTORY		
Chapter 5: From Settlement to Independence: 1607–1776 • Introduction: *Colonial Americans: Who Were They?* • General Interest: *Famous Colonial Americans* • Academic: *The Road to Rebellion*	• Guessing the Meanings of New Words: Using an Explanation in the Next Sentence • Previewing: Scanning for Years • Previewing: Scanning for Events • Making a Timeline	• Strategy: Writing a Summary • Focus: Paragraph Summarizing a Reading from the Chapter
Chapter 6: A Changing Nation: 1850–1900 • Introduction: *Voices from the Past* • General Interest: *The End of the Frontier* • Academic: *Changing Patterns of Immigration*	• Interpreting Graphs • Finding Specific Support • Using a T-chart • Understanding Cause and Effect	• Strategy: Writing a Paragraph of Comparison • Focus: Paragraph Comparing a Pair of Pictures

The Mechanics of Writing	Critical Thinking Strategies	Test-Taking Strategies
UNIT 2 BIOLOGY		
• Simple Past • Combining Ideas • *When* and *Because* • Adverbials of Time • Using Direct and Indirect Objects • Using Articles: *A, An,* and *The*	• Applying Information • Classifying	• Understanding Pronouns
• Count and Noncount Food Nouns • *Too Much* and *Too Many* • *A Lot Of* and *Not Enough* • Cause and Effect with *If (not) . . . will*	• Forming an Opinion • Previewing: Figures and Tables	• Checking Your Work
UNIT 3 U.S. HISTORY		
• *Can* and *Could* • Causatives: *Force* and *Make* • Summary Writing: Condensing	• Using a Venn Diagram to Show Similarities and Differences	• Paraphrasing
• Transition Words of Contrast • Using *There + Be* • Using Quotations to Support General Statements	• Using a T-chart • Finding Specific Support	• Finding Unstated Details

Welcome

Quest Second Edition prepares students for academic success. The series features two complementary strands—*Reading and Writing* and *Listening and Speaking*—each with four levels. The integrated Quest program provides robust scaffolding to support and accelerate each student's journey from exploring general interest topics to mastering academic content.

New second edition features

- New *Intro* level providing on-ramp to Books 1-3

- Redesigned, larger format with captivating photos

- Expanded focus on critical thinking skills

- Addition of research paper to *Reading and Writing* strand

- New unit-ending *Vocabulary Workshops* and end-of-book Academic Word List (AWL)

- Expanded video program (VHS/DVD) with new lecture and updated social language footage

- EZ Test® CD-ROM test generator for all *Reading and Writing* titles

- Test-Taking strategy boxes that highlight skills needed for success on the new TOEFL® iBT

- Teacher's Editions with activity-by-activity procedural notes, expansion activities, and tests

Captivating photos and graphics capture students' attention while introducing each academic topic.

U N I T 1

BUSINESS

Chapter 1
Career Planning

Chapter 2
The Free Enterprise System

AFTER READING

A. MAIN IDEA Discuss this question with a partner:
• How does McDonald's try to adapt to the food preferences of different cultures?

B. FINDING DETAILS Use information in the reading to match the food preferences to the countries. Write the correct letters on the lines.

_____ **1.** mutton   **a.** India

_____ **2.** salmon   **b.** Norway

_____ **3.** teriyaki   **c.** Turkey

_____ **4.** yogurt   **d.** Japan

Reading Strategy

Understanding Italics

As you learned in Chapter 3, writers use italics for different reasons. One reason writers use italics is for foreign words.

Example: Many French dishes use a *bordelaise* sauce.

Writers also use italics to stress important words, such as words that don't show opposite ideas.

Example: Jason doesn't like Chinese food, but he *loves* Korean food.

C. UNDERSTANDING ITALICS Look back at the reading on page 95. Find words in italics to answer the questions below. Write the answers on the lines.

1. What is the name for a popular chilled yogurt drink in Turkey? _____

2. What is the opposite of something that is foreign? _____

Critical Thinking Strategy

Forming an Opinion

As you read, try to form your own opinion about the ideas in a passage. When you form an opinion, have reasons to support it. This helps you to focus on and to remember important information.

Example: While reading the passage on page 95 you think, "McDonald's seems like a smart company because it thinks about the local market."

Strategy-based approach develops reading, writing, critical thinking, and test-taking skills needed for academic success.

Three high-interest reading selections in each chapter introduce students to the course content most frequently required by universities.

READING

Read about two unusual animals. As you read, think about these questions:
• What did the octopus learn?
• Why is the tiger unusual?

Animal Tales

Octopus Intelligence

With its eight powerful arms, an octopus can swim backwards or pull itself over rocks on the ocean floor. An octopus is very strong, but is it intelligent? People at the Hellabrunn Zoo, in Germany, might have an opinion about this.

Glass jars do not exist in the ocean, the natural environment of an octopus, so you might not expect an octopus to know how to open one. However, at the Hellabrunn Zoo, an octopus named Frieda had the motivation to learn how to open a jar. The motivation was food. Frieda watched her human keepers as they opened glass jars with food inside. From watching them, she learned how to twist off the lid and reach inside for the food.

Interestingly, she will not open just *any* jar. She doesn't open jars that contain fish. According to a representative of the zoo, "She'll open only jars containing her favorite foods, such as shrimp, clams, and crabs."

An octopus

Brother Tiger

How much of an animal's behavior is from nature (biology)? How much is from nurture (life experience)? Can nurture change an animal's nature? Can early life experience have an influence on an adult animal?

You might think that for a hungry tiger, a baby pig would naturally be lunch. However, for Saimai, a two-year-old Bengal tiger, piglets are not lunch. According to *Best Friends Magazine*, Saimai plays with them as if they were his brothers. That's because when he was a cub, Saimai grew up with piglets. He thought that *their* mother was *his* mother. She suckled him—fed him milk—while she was suckling her real babies.

Will this behavior continue or will Saimai suddenly return to his instinctive nature? Nobody knows the answer, but maybe those piglets shouldn't get *too* close to their "brother," just in case.

Source: *Best Friends Magazine*

Saimai

CHAPTER 3 Animal Behavior **71**

READING

Read about animal behavior. As you read, highlight the topic sentence—the first sentence—in each paragraph. Think about this question:
• How do animals learn?

How Do Animals Learn?

Behavior is the way that animals act. For example, how do they get food or take care of their young? How do they find a place to live or protect themselves from danger? Behavior is either **innate** or **learned**.

Innate Behavior

Much behavior is **innate**; that is, animals are *born* with it. Their genes determine the animals' behavior. In other words, the behavior is a biological inheritance. Some innate behaviors are simple, such as a **reflex** or a **fight-or-flight response**. What happens if something suddenly passes in front of your eyes? You blink—that is, you quickly close and open your eyes. This is a reflex. You have no control over it. Think about a time when you were very afraid. Your heart began to beat faster, and you began to breathe faster. Maybe your body started to shake. You were having a fight-or-flight response. Your body was preparing for danger. You had no control over this behavior. Both a reflex and a fight-or-flight response are simple and quick.

Another, more complex, kind of innate behavior is **instinct**. Two kinds of instinctive behavior are **territoriality** and **migration**. Many animals have a strong sense of territory—a place that they "own." For example, a male sea lion protects his area of beach by attacking other male sea lions that come onto it. This is territoriality. Another instinctive behavior, migration, is the movement of animals from one part of the world to another. For example, every fall, many birds fly from North America to South America because there is more food in South America during the winter. They migrate back north in the spring. Whales also migrate seasonally.

Territoriality: Male sea lions fight for territory

Migration: Geese fly south for the winter

CHAPTER 3 Animal Behavior **79**

Gradual curve in each chapter from general interest to academic content supports students as they engage in increasingly more difficult material.

Discussion, pair-work, and group-work activities **scaffold the learning process** as students move from general interest to academic content.

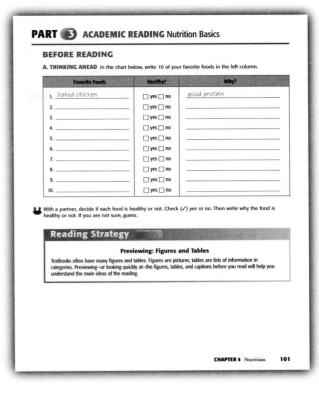

BEFORE READING

A. THINKING AHEAD In the chart below, write 10 of your favorite foods in the left column.

Favorite Foods	Healthy?	Why?
1. baked chicken	☐ yes ☐ no	good protein
2.	☐ yes ☐ no	
3.	☐ yes ☐ no	
4.	☐ yes ☐ no	
5.	☐ yes ☐ no	
6.	☐ yes ☐ no	
7.	☐ yes ☐ no	
8.	☐ yes ☐ no	
9.	☐ yes ☐ no	
10.	☐ yes ☐ no	

With a partner, decide if each food is healthy or not. Check (✓) *yes* or *no*. Then write why the food is healthy or not. If you are not sure, guess.

Reading Strategy

Previewing: Figures and Tables

Textbooks often have many figures and tables. Figures are pictures; tables are lists of information in categories. Previewing—or looking quickly at—the figures, tables, and captions before you read will help you understand the main ideas of the reading.

UNIT ❶ VOCABULARY WORKSHOP

Review vocabulary that you learned in Chapters 1 and 2.

A. MATCHING Match the definitions to the words. Write the correct letters on the lines.

_a_ **1.** goods	**a.** products to sell
_____ **2.** values	**b.** too much of something
_____ **3.** lifestyle	**c.** small parts of a population
_____ **4.** major	**d.** a way of living life
_____ **5.** minorities	**e.** things that are important to your life
_____ **6.** motivation	**f.** one's main area of study at college
_____ **7.** myth	**g.** popular activities or fashions
_____ **8.** rehabilitation	**h.** treatment to improve a problem
_____ **9.** surplus	**i.** an incorrect idea
_____ **10.** trends	**j.** reasons for doing something

B. TRUE OR FALSE? Which sentences are true? Which are false? Fill in Ⓣ for *True* or Ⓕ for *False*.

1. An animator is a kind of politician. Ⓣ ●
2. A college career counselor helps you choose a major or prepare for a career. Ⓣ Ⓕ
3. A consumer is someone who buys something. Ⓣ Ⓕ
4. Job-switching means keeping one job for life. Ⓣ Ⓕ
5. People who are between the ages of 13 and 18 are tweens. Ⓣ Ⓕ
6. Market segments are groups of individuals or organizations with similar characteristics. Ⓣ Ⓕ
7. A shortage is too much of something. Ⓣ Ⓕ
8. Medical illustrators communicate medical or scientific information. Ⓣ Ⓕ

Unit-Ending *Vocabulary Workshops* **reinforce key unit vocabulary** that appears on the Academic Word List (AWL).

Expanded video program for the *Listening and Speaking* titles now includes mini-lectures to build comprehension and note-taking skills, and updated social language scenes to develop conversation skills.

Audio program selections are indicated with this icon ⌒ and include recordings of all lectures, conversations, pronunciation and intonation activities, and reading selections.

Teacher's Edition provides activity-by-activity teaching suggestions, expansion activities, tests, and special TOEFL® iBT preparation notes

EZ Test® CD-ROM test generator for the *Reading and Writing* titles allows teachers to create customized tests in a matter of minutes.

Getting Started

Discuss these questions:

- Look at the picture. Where is the woman?
- How much do you read every week?
- What are some ways you can improve your reading skills?
- What are some ways you can improve your writing skills?

INTRODUCTION TO READING

Reading is a very important part of college*. In college, you need to read a lot. You read to get new ideas and information. You read to learn new vocabulary. You read to discover your own opinions. In fact, you usually do a lot of reading before you write anything in college.

In this book, you will read and discuss three readings in each chapter before you begin to write a paragraph. The book gives you many suggestions on how to improve your reading skills. This will help you to become a better reader.

Below is a short reading. You will understand most of it, but you probably won't understand everything. What is a good way to read it? First, read it silently. Reading out loud will make you read more slowly. Second, read the whole passage without stopping.

*Americans usually use the word *college* to mean higher education in general. It can mean college or university.

Getting the Most Out of a Textbook

In some countries, students' textbooks are in pristine—perfect—condition. Students cover them carefully in plastic. They turn the pages carefully. They never fold the corner of a page up or down. And they never, never write in their textbooks. The situation is quite different in the United States. American
5 students' textbooks are a mess. Students absolutely deface them—but not because these students are messy people.

Most American college students need to be efficient readers. This is necessary because full-time students probably have to read several hundred pages every week. They don't have time to read a chapter three or four times. They need to
10 extract as much information as possible from the first or second reading.

An essential study skill is knowing how to mark a book. Students mark the main ideas (most important information) and important details (small points) with a highlighter—a yellow or blue or orange pen that lets you write over words but still read them. Some students mark new words in a different color. Most students
15 also use a pen or pencil to write questions or notes in the margins.

Marking a book is a useful skill, but it's important to do it right. First, read a chapter with one highlighter in your hand and others next to you. Second, read a whole paragraph before you mark anything. Then don't mark too much; usually, you'll mark about 10 percent (%) of a reading. Third, decide on your own
20 system for marking. For example, maybe you'll mark main ideas in yellow, important details in blue, and new words in orange. Maybe you'll put question marks (?) in the margin when you don't understand something.

When your chapter is a rainbow of markings, you don't have to read all of it again before an exam. Instead, you just need to review your marks, and you can
25 save a lot of time.

You probably understood most of this reading. But what can you do about the new vocabulary?

Reading Strategy

Guessing the Meaning from Context

You often find new words in textbooks. But it's important not to use a dictionary for every new word. Instead, try to guess the word from its context–the sentence or paragraph that the word is in.

Example: In some countries, students' textbooks are in pristine–perfect–condition.

What does *pristine* mean? Look at the rest of the sentence. The dashes and the word *perfect* tell you that *pristine* = *perfect*.

Looking for and understanding dashes is just one way to guess the meaning of a new word. You'll see many more in this book.

Sometimes you don't need to know the meaning of a new word because the word isn't important. Also, you can understand the main ideas of a reading without knowing the meaning of every word in it.

Example: An essential study skill is knowing how to mark a book.

Do you need to know the meaning of *essential*? No. The important words are *study skills*. An essential study skill is an important study skill, but you don't need to know this to understand the sentence.

Look at the diagram below. It shows you what to do when you see a new word. First, ask yourself: Can I guess the meaning of the word from its context?

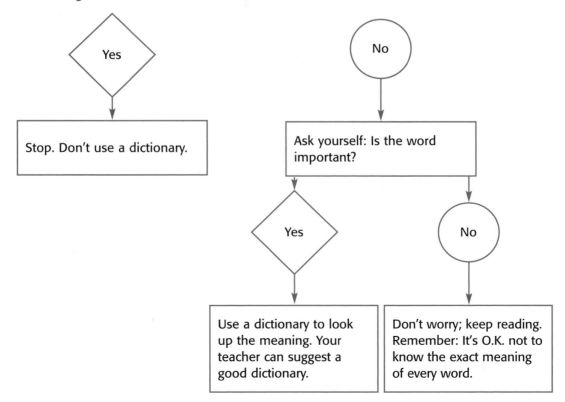

A. GUESSING THE MEANING FROM CONTEXT Reread the passage on page 2. As you read, look for words that you don't know. When you find one, ask yourself the questions from the diagram on page 3.

Write the new words you find in the chart below. Fill in the bubbles of your answers to the questions.

New Word: _____	Can I guess? Is it important?	YES YES	NO NO
New Word: _____	Can I guess? Is it important?	YES YES	NO NO
New Word: _____	Can I guess? Is it important?	YES YES	NO NO
New Word: _____	Can I guess? Is it important?	YES YES	NO NO
New Word: _____	Can I guess? Is it important?	YES YES	NO NO
New Word: _____	Can I guess? Is it important?	YES YES	NO NO
New Word: _____	Can I guess? Is it important?	YES YES	NO NO

B. GUESSING THE MEANING FROM CONTEXT Which new words from Activity A can you guess? Write the words and your guesses on the lines.

New Word: _____   My guess: _____

New Word: _____   My guess: _____

New Word: _____   My guess: _____

New Word: _____   My guess: _____

New Word: _____   My guess: _____

New Word: _____   My guess: _____

Keeping a Word Journal

A Word Journal is a notebook for new words. When you learn the meaning of a new word, write it down in a special notebook—a notebook just for words—or one section in your three-ring binder. Writing down a new word, its meaning, and the part of speech helps you remember it. Also, if you forget what the new words mean or how to spell them, you can look them up in your Word Journal. It's like a personal dictionary.

Get your special Word Journal notebook before you start Chapter 1 of this book. Each chapter has a Word Journal assignment.

Here is an example of a Word Journal entry:

January 18

1. pristine	perfect
adj	Textbooks are in _____ condition.

Understanding Parts of Speech

Before you look up a word in the dictionary, you need to know its part of speech. The part of speech is the form of the word: noun, verb, adjective, adverb, etc. A dictionary uses abbreviations for the parts of speech: n = noun; v = verb; adj = adjective; adv = adverb.

A noun is a word for a person, place, thing, or situation.   **Examples: student, college, textbook**

A verb is usually an action word.   **Examples: is, are, cover, turn**

An adjective modifies (describes) a noun.   **Examples: necessary, new, short**

An adverb modifies an adjective or verb.   **Examples: carefully, easily, never**

Many words can have two or three different parts of speech. An easy way to decide the part of speech is to look at the context—the sentence that the word is in. In the following sentences, notice that you can decide the part of speech of the "new words" (XXs) from the context.

Examples: She picked up her **XX**.
(**Noun:** It's after the possessive pronoun *her*.)

She picked up her **XX** book.
(**Adjective:** It's before a noun.)

After she picked up her book, she **XX** it.
(**Verb:** It comes after the subject, *she*, and in this example, it also has an object, *it*.)

She **XX** picked up her book. OR: She picked up her book **XX**.
(**Adverb:** It modifies the verb, *picked up*.)

She picked up her **XX** heavy book.
(**Adverb:** It modifies an adjective, *heavy*.)

C. UNDERSTANDING PARTS OF SPEECH Write the part of speech of the words in these sentences. Don't use a dictionary.

1. Taylor's textbook looks quite colorful.

   looks = _____

   quite = _____

   colorful = _____

2. Students absolutely deface their textbooks.

   students = _____

   absolutely = _____

   deface = _____

   textbooks = _____

3. An essential study skill is knowing how to mark a book.

   essential = _____

   skill = _____

   mark = _____

Reading Strategy

Understanding Parts of Speech: Suffixes

Another way to decide the part of speech is from the suffix (the ending) of the word. Here are some common suffixes.

Suffixes for Nouns	Suffixes for Adjectives	Suffixes for Adverbs
-tion	-less	-ly
-sion	-ful	-ily
-ence	-ent	-fully
-ance	-ant	
-er, -or, -ist	-al	
-ment	-ible	
-ness	-able	

D. UNDERSTANDING PARTS OF SPEECH: SUFFIXES Decide the part of speech of each word below from its suffix. Write *n* (noun), *adj* (adjective), or *adv* (adverb).

1. _____ reader

2. _____ usually

3. _____ possible

4. _____ difference

5. _____ situational

6. _____ condition

7. _____ beautifully

8. _____ careless

9. _____ teacher

10. _____ possibly

11. _____ efficient

12. _____ careful

13. _____ question

14. _____ efficiently

15. _____ questionable

16. _____ discussion

17. _____ happiness

18. _____ distant

19. _____ assignment

20. _____ importance

Reading Strategy

Using a Dictionary: Alphabetizing

When you need to use a dictionary, you want to be able to find words quickly. Words in a dictionary are in alphabetical order.

Example: These words are in alphabetical order.

after
cover
necessary
write

In a group of words, if the first letter is the same, look at the second letter. If the first and second letters are the same, look at the third letter, and so on.

Example: These words are in alphabetical order.

still
student
study

E. ALPHABETIZING As quickly as possible, put the words in each group in alphabetical order. Number the words from 1 to 9.

Group 1	Group 2	Group 3
_____ paragraph	_____ skill	_____ need
_____ mark	_____ third	_____ must
__1__ decide	_____ review	_____ efficient
_____ full-time	_____ difficult	_____ messy
_____ rainbow	_____ pen	_____ essential
_____ from	_____ reader	_____ much
_____ probably	_____ several	_____ maybe
__9__ right	_____ passage	_____ never
_____ first	_____ different	_____ margin

Reading Strategy

Recognizing Main Ideas and Details

In both reading and writing, it's important to know the difference between main ideas and details. A main idea is a general idea. It tells you the central idea. A detail is specific information. It supports (explains or gives reasons and examples for) a main idea.

Good writers think about the difference between main ideas and details as they write. They put main ideas first and details next. They organize their ideas like this:

Main Idea
    Detail 1
    Detail 2
    Etc.

This makes their writing easier for readers to understand.

Examples: Students have a lot of homework.
(This sentence talks about a main idea: homework.)

They often have to read several hundred textbook pages a week.
(This sentence gives a detail: an example of homework.)

They also have to write several long papers.
(This sentence also gives a detail: another example of homework.)

F. RECOGNIZING MAIN IDEAS AND DETAILS The following groups of ideas are mixed up. Each has one main idea and two details. Read the sentences. Find the main idea and put a *M* next to it. Put a *D* next to each detail sentence.

1. _____ College textbooks have a lot of new ideas.

   _____ College textbooks can be difficult.

   ___D___ College textbooks have many new words and expressions.

2. _____ College students need notebooks.

   _____ College students need highlighters.

   _____ College students need a lot of supplies to do good work.

3. _____ Good writers organize their ideas logically.

   _____ Good writers help readers understand their ideas.

   _____ Good writers explain their ideas completely.

Reading Strategy

Recognizing Phrases and Clauses

In both reading and writing, it's important to understand the difference between a phrase and a clause.

A phrase is a group of two or more words. It is not a sentence. There are different kinds of phrases.

Examples:

Noun Phrases	Verb Phrases	Prepositional Phrases
messy people	turn the page	in the margin
a short reading	get new ideas	with a pencil
study skills	mark a book	after the reading

A clause has at least a subject, a verb with a tense, and (if necessary) an object. An independent clause with a capital letter at the beginning and a period at the end is a sentence.

Examples: students absolutely **deface their books** (Independent clause)
          S   V   O

      Students absolutely deface their books. (Sentence)

G. RECOGNIZING PHRASES AND CLAUSES Identify these groups of words. Write *P* for phrases and *C* for clauses. Then change the clauses into sentences.

1. _____C_____ they marked the paragraph   They marked the paragraph.

2. _____ marking a book

3. _____ with a yellow highlighter pen

4. _____ students from many different countries

5. _____ it is useful

6. _____ they don't have time

7. _____ from the first or second reading

Reading Strategy

Recognizing Topics and Main Ideas

In both reading and writing, it's important to recognize the topic of a paragraph and the main idea of a paragraph. A topic is a word or phrase that states what a paragraph is about. The main idea is a complete sentence that says something about the topic. (Remember, a complete sentence has at least a subject and a verb.)

Examples: The condition of textbooks **(topic)**
            In some countries, students' textbooks are in pristine condition. **(main idea)**

The first item, *the condition of textbooks*, is a topic. It isn't a complete sentence. The second item is a main idea—a complete sentence that says something about the topic. (It's the main idea of the first paragraph from the reading on page 2.)

H. RECOGNIZING TOPICS AND MAIN IDEAS Identify these groups of words. Write *T* for topics and *MI* for main ideas. Remember, a complete sentence has at least a subject and a verb.

1. _____T_____ textbooks

2. _____ getting the most out of a textbook

3. _____ good readers

4. _____ good readers organize their ideas logically

5. _____ how to read a book

6. _____ a highlighter pen is an important tool

7. _____ highlighter pens as important tools

INTRODUCTION TO WRITING

In this section, you are going to write a paragraph. As you write, you are going to learn a **process**—a way of doing something—that makes writing easier. The writing process has five main steps: Choosing a Topic, Planning your Paragraph, Writing the Paragraph, Editing, and Rewriting. When you finish the five steps, you will have a good paragraph.

The writing assignment is to write one paragraph to answer these questions:
• What is your favorite book? Why is it your favorite?

Writing Strategy

Step A. Choosing a Topic

Often when you write for school, you get to choose your own topic. It's important to choose carefully. Choose a topic that is easy for you to write about. An easy topic is a topic that:

• is interesting to you
• you know well
• you have information about

STEP A. CHOOSING A TOPIC Here are some possible topics for the writing assignment. In this case, they are about specific books. Write your answers on the lines. Then add some ideas of your own.

• a book that I read last summer: _____ The History of Xenrovia _____

• a book that I read when I was a child: _____

• a book that I am reading right now: _____

• a textbook: _____

• other books that I have read:

_____ : _____
      (Type of book)   **(Title)**

_____ : _____
      (Type of book)   **(Title)**

_____ : _____
      (Type of book)   **(Title)**

Now answer these questions.

1. Which book from the list on page 11 is the most interesting for you to write about?

   _____

2. Which book do you know well?

   _____

3. Which book do you have some information about?

   _____

4. Which is your favorite book?

   _____

5. Which book will you choose to write about?

   _____

Writing Strategy

Step B. Planning Your Paragraph

Planning your paragraph means getting ideas and organizing them. You can get ideas for your paragraph from readings, discussion with other students, and thinking. As you plan your paragraph, take notes.

There are many ways to organize ideas in a paragraph. You will learn them in this book. However, all good paragraphs have a main idea and several **supporting ideas**—details that support the main idea. When you plan your paragraph, think of your main idea. Then make a list of reasons that support it.

Look at this example of main and supporting ideas about a favorite book:
    My favorite book is *The History of Xenrovia*. (**main idea**)
    The History of Xenrovia is very well written. (**detail**)
    The History of Xenrovia has beautiful pictures. (**detail**)

The first sentence is the main idea. It answers the question: What is your favorite book? It's narrow enough to talk about in one paragraph. The second and third sentences are details. They give examples of why *The History of Xenrovia* is the writer's favorite book.

STEP B. PLANNING YOUR PARAGRAPH Answer these questions.

1. What is your favorite book?

   _____

2. What is one reason that this is your favorite book?

   _____

What is an example of this reason?

_____

3. What is another reason that this is your favorite book?

_____

What is an example of this reason?

_____

4. What is one more reason that this is your favorite book?

_____

What is an example of this reason?

_____

Writing Strategy

Step C. Writing the Paragraph

The next step is to put the sentences that you wrote from your notes into a first draft of your paragraph. A paragraph has a main idea sentence and several sentences that support the main idea. Write complete sentences and connect them with transition words (such as *for example* or *another reason*). Indent the first sentence in the paragraph, and end each sentence with a period.

What does a first draft look like? It might be missing some information, it might have some information that is not in a logical order, or it might have some grammar or spelling mistakes.

Look at this example of a first draft:

My favorite book is *The History of Xenrovia*. It's my favorite because its very well written. Many history books are boring but *The History of Xenrovia* includes interesting stories about the important people in the history of the country. *The History of Xenrovia* also has wonderful pictures. For example there is beautiful fotographs of the capital city Xenoville at night and during a rainstorm. Another reason that *The History of Xenrovia* is my favorite book is that it's very complete It begins with stories about the first people who lived in the area and it ends with informations about life in the country today. I still have many friends in Xenrovia.

As you can see, this first draft is quite good. However, the first sentence in the paragraph is not indented. Also, there are a few grammar and spelling mistakes. (Can you find them?) Finally, the last sentence isn't really necessary.

STEP C. WRITING THE PARAGRAPH Use your notes from Step B (pages 12–13). On a separate piece of paper, write complete sentences in paragraph form. You might make some mistakes, but don't worry about them at this point.

Writing Strategy

Step D. Editing

It's important to check your own work for mistakes before you give it to a teacher. Checking your own work helps you to be an independent writer. You won't always have a teacher to help you! Editing helps you write better drafts before your teacher even sees your work. For each assignment in this book, you will edit your own work.

When you edit look for:
- organization (no unnecessary sentences; correct order of ideas)
- form (indentation; margins)
- spelling
- grammar

STEP D. EDITING Read the paragraph you wrote and answer these questions.

1. Is the paragraph form correct? Did you indent the first line?

_____

2. Is there a main idea statement about your favorite book?

_____

3. Are there sentences that support your main idea?

_____

4. Are there specific examples for each supporting idea?

_____

5. Are there transition words that connect the sentences?

_____

6. Is there any information that doesn't fit?

_____

7. Are there any spelling or grammar mistakes?

_____

Step E: Rewriting

After you edit your paragraph, rewrite it. Try to write it without the mistakes. Ask yourself: Do I have only one main idea? Did I support my main idea? Did I capitalize and punctuate correctly? Is my paragraph free of spelling and grammar mistakes?

Here is an example of a second draft of the paragraph on page 13. The mistakes have been corrected.

My favorite book is *The History of Xenrovia.* It's my favorite because it's very well written. Many history books are boring, but *The History of Xenrovia.* includes interesting stories about the important people in the history of the country. *The History of Xenrovia* also has wonderful pictures. For example, there are beautiful photographs of the capital city, Xenoville, at night and during a rainstorm. Another reason that *The History of Xenrovia* is my favorite book is that it's very complete. It begins with stories about the first people who lived in the area, and it ends with information about life in the country today.

STEP E. REWRITING Use the answers from Step D to help you rewrite your paragraph.

UNIT 1

BUSINESS

Chapter 1
Career Planning

Chapter 2
The Free Enterprise System

Career Planning

Discuss these questions:
- Look at the picture. What is each man's job?
- Which job would you like more? Why?
- What job do you want in the future?
- Read the chapter title. What do you think the chapter will be about?

BEFORE READING

Danielle prepares food at a restaurant.

Michelle does experiments in a laboratory.

Max designs toys for a toy company.

Campbell presents the news on television.

THINKING AHEAD Look at the pictures of people at work. Answer these questions with a partner.

1. What are the people in the pictures doing? What might their job titles be?

2. What do you think each person's personality is like?

3. Match each word below to one or more of the jobs in the pictures.

   difficult   easy   exciting   fun   interesting   stressful

   Example: Max's job looks fun.

READING

Read about cool jobs. As you read, think about these questions:
• How did the people get their cool jobs? What are their qualifications (experience and skills)?

Cool Jobs

It's time to think about a career. A career is work that you train for and do for most of your life. For some people, it's easy to choose a career. They get ideas from relatives or friends or from watching the people around them, such as teachers or doctors. But for some people, it's difficult to choose a career. They're afraid of making a mistake.

5   They don't want just *any* job. They especially don't want a boring job. Does work have to be dull? Does it have to be ordinary? Can't work be *extra*ordinary? Can't it be cool—fun and exciting? The answer is *yes*. Here are

10   some people with cool jobs.

Peter Lind, ice cream taster

Peter Lind is a professional ice cream taster. His real job title is Flavor Development Specialist. He works for Ben & Jerry's Ice Cream, in Waterbury, Vermont. He creates
15   new ice cream flavors for the company. He gets ideas, makes samples, and tries them out. He also thinks about ice cream flavors that other people will like. Lind worked as a chef and a baker before he worked with Ben
20   & Jerry's. A good ice cream flavor developer must have culinary (food preparation) training or experience, be creative, and like ice cream!

Anthony Marinaccio operates the Cyclone Roller Coaster at the Coney Island
25   amusement park in New York. Marinaccio grew up on Coney Island. As a child, he played at the beach and rode the amusement park rides every day. As a teenager, he worked at the park and did many different jobs. He had fun, and he learned a lot about his future job. Today, Marinaccio greets and seats roller coaster riders. How did he get the job? Luck and friendship played a part. One day, over 25 years ago, when
30   he didn't have a job, Marinaccio met his childhood friend Gerald Menditto on the street. Menditto is the Cyclone's operations manager, and he remembered that Marinaccio was a hard worker with a good sense of humor (he likes to laugh). He offered Marinaccio a job, and the two men have worked together on the Cyclone ever since. Today, Marinaccio still enjoys riding on the roller coaster.

Bruce Shelley, computer game designer

35 **Bruce Shelley** designs computer games for Ensemble Studios. He has created many games, including the popular *Age of Empires. Age of Empires* is an online strategy game about world history. Shelley

40 designed paper and board games before he started designing computer games. He believes that games should be both entertaining and educational. Shelley is

45 curious, likes to solve puzzles, and has a strong interest in history. He is not a computer programmer himself, but many other game designers know computer programming, game theory, and/or 3D computer graphics design.

50 **Kitty Black Perkins** is a fashion designer. But she doesn't do what you think she does. Her model is over forty years old, world famous, and about 12 inches (30.5 centimeters) tall. Perkins designs clothes for Barbie, Mattel Toys' popular fashion doll. Every year, Perkins designs hundreds of new fashions for Barbie and the other dolls in the Barbie collection. Perkins has

55 designed Barbie fashions for Mattel for over 20 years. In addition, she created Mattel's first African-American fashion doll, Shani. According to Mattel, a Barbie designer must be creative and have experience in the design

60 industry.

Francie Berger plays with toys all day long. She's a professional LEGO designer. Berger creates huge LEGO structures. The company uses them at stores and toy shows.

65 Berger has played with LEGOs since she was three years old. She studied architecture at Virginia Polytechnic Institute. One day, Berger heard a guest speaker talk about toy design. She decided to combine her architecture

70 degree with her love of LEGOs and become a toy designer. She gave LEGO, a Danish company, the idea to open a U.S. design operation. They agreed. She also gave them the idea to hire her. Berger loves her job. She

75 suggests that future toy designers go to college and get art-related experience.

Francie Berger, LEGO designer

AFTER READING

A. CHECK YOUR UNDERSTANDING Write information from the reading in the chart. Write the people's jobs. Describe what they do and their qualifications in your own words.

Names	Jobs	What They Do	Qualifications
Peter Lind	ice cream taster	develops new ice cream flavors	has culinary experience, likes ice cream, is creative
Anthony Marinaccio			
Bruce Shelley			
Kitty Black Perkins			
Francie Berger			

Critical Thinking Strategy

Applying Your Knowledge to New Situations

Using what you already know in new situations is an important critical thinking skill. It helps you remember new information.

Example: **You read:** Peter Lind went to culinary school.
You think: My friend Cindy went to culinary school. She said it was very difficult. She had to take math classes.

B. USING YOUR KNOWLEDGE With a partner, look at the job titles in the box. Make sure that you understand each one.

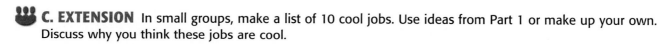

| a. actor* | c. chef | e. news reporter |
| b. architect | d. clothing designer | f. scientist |

Now read the sentences. Match the jobs from the box to the people and their qualifications. Write the letters of the correct jobs on the lines.

_____c_____ **1.** Roberto has worked in restaurants since he was 16 years old. He went to culinary school, and he enjoys developing new dishes.

_____ **2.** Candy is interested in world events. She likes to talk to people, and she's a good writer.

_____ **3.** In high school, Rachel was in every play. She studies drama in college.

_____ **4.** Chris likes to do experiments. She is interested in nature. She collected insects when she was a child.

_____ **5.** Tomas learned to sew when he was six. He helped his mother make her clothes. He went to design school.

_____ **6.** David is creative. He played with LEGOs when he was a child. He likes to design buildings.

*In American English people use *actor* to refer to both men and women. It is also common to use *actress* for women.

C. EXTENSION In small groups, make a list of 10 cool jobs. Use ideas from Part 1 or make up your own. Discuss why you think these jobs are cool.

Now discuss the perfect job for you. (In other words, your **ideal** job.) Answer these questions.

1. Do you have a job now? What is it?

2. What is your ideal job?

3. Is it fun? Why? Why not?

4. What are the qualifications for this job?

PART ② GENERAL INTEREST READING
Finding the Job That's Right for You

BEFORE READING

Reading Strategy

Connecting with the Topic

The title usually tells you the topic of a reading. Read the title and think about the topic before you read a passage. Try to connect your interests and experience with the topic. Connecting with the topic will help you to focus as you read. For example, the title of the next reading is "Finding the Job That's Right for You." To connect with the topic you might think about your ideal job. You could also think about someone you know who really likes his or her job.

A. THINKING AHEAD To help you connect with the topic of the next reading, discuss these questions with a partner.

1. Do you know people who love their jobs? Tell your partner about them.

2. Why do they like their jobs? What kind of people are they?

Reading Strategy

Guessing the Meanings of New Words: Definitions after *Be* or *Means*

When you don't know the meaning of a new word, you don't always need to use a dictionary. Sometimes you can find a definition of the new word right in the same sentence. Sentences with definitions usually follow the verb *be* (*is* or *are*) or *means.*

Example: Your **values are** things that are important to you in life.

B. GUESSING THE MEANINGS OF NEW WORDS As you read the next passage, look for meanings of new words after *be* or *means.*

READING

Read about how to find the right job. As you read, think about the answer to the question below. When you find the answer, mark it with a highlighter. (You will need to highlight more than one sentence.)

• How do you find a job that you will love?

Finding the Job That's Right for You

Most people want to love their jobs. They want to be excited about their jobs. They want to feel happy about getting out of bed in the morning and
5 starting each day. How do you find a job like this?

People Who Love Their Jobs

First of all, it helps to know something about people who love their jobs. Who are they? What are they like?
10 What's important to them? Richard I. Fein decided to find out. He works at the Isenberg School of Management at the University of Massachusetts. He also wrote the book *100 Great Jobs and*
15 *How to Get Them.* Fein interviewed 100 people who love their jobs. He met a woman who designs the boxes Barbie dolls come in, an FBI agent who investigates crime in big companies,
20 and the manager of a women's basketball team. All of these people love their jobs.

The people in Fein's study share certain characteristics. First, they feel
25 they are doing what they do best. Second, they are doing what interests them. And finally, they believe that their work is important. Fein found another interesting thing about these people:
30 money isn't very important to them.

How to Find the Job That's Right for You

Most career counselors agree: to find a job that you will love, you need
to do a self-assessment exercise. Self-assessment means learning about
35 yourself. In fact, to find a job that's right for you, you must get to know yourself very well. Self-assessment will help you discover what you do best and what interests you. And most
40 importantly, it will help you discover your values. Values are things that are important to you in life. There are many tools that you can use in this self-assessment process. There are books,
45 tests, and classes. They all help you answer these three questions: What am I good at? What do I like to do? What are my values?

The first task is to find out what you
50 do best. Start by thinking about the classes that you took in school. What classes did you like the most? In which classes did you get the best grades? What kinds of tests did you do well on?
55 The answers to these questions can help you discover what you do best. For example, people who do well in language and literature classes probably have good communication skills. They
60 might enjoy a job in journalism. People who are good at math and science might think about engineering. And people who excel in (are very good at) art might consider graphic design.

65 However, sometimes you do well in a subject, but you don't enjoy it. For example, you might get high scores on math exams, but you really don't like math. The next step is to think about

70 what you enjoy doing. What clubs do
you belong to? What sports do you play?
What are your hobbies? Your free time
activities can be a clue to your true
interests. For example, Francie Berger
75 liked playing with LEGOs and became a
toy designer. Bruce Shelley always loved
playing games; he became a computer
game designer. When choosing the right
job, don't forget to think about what you
80 *hate* doing. Some people hate public
speaking (speaking in front of a lot of
people). People who hate public speaking
probably shouldn't consider jobs such as
teaching or broadcast journalism
85 because they involve speaking in front
of large groups.

Campbell Brown works in broadcast journalism.

Finally, you need to think about
your values. Most people work 40 hours
a week or more. You don't want to be
90 doing something you don't believe in or
you think is wrong. When thinking
about your values, think about the
following: Do you want to help others?
Do you want to improve the
95 environment? What are your politics? Is
it important to work with or for people
who think as you do? Lifestyle is
important, too. Your lifestyle is the way
that you live your life. Is a healthy
100 lifestyle important to you? Do you want
a job that isn't stressful? And finally,
don't forget to think about how
important money is to you.

The answers to these questions will
105 help you discover the job that is right
for you. For example, a computer game
designer might think education is
important. So he or she probably
wouldn't want to work for a company
110 that makes games that are silly, violent,
or just for fun. A doll designer who is
African-American might want to work
for a company that makes toys for
children from many different cultures
115 or races.

Putting It All Together

After you've answered all the big
questions, the next step is finding jobs
that match your profile. Your profile is a
list of characteristics that describes you.
120 There may be several possibilities. For
example, let's consider Mary, a young
woman who does well in languages and
art. In her free time, she enjoys
photography, cooking, and playing
125 soccer. Mary enjoys helping people and
being part of a team. She might
consider a job in the media, food
service or hospitality (the restaurant
or hotel business), teaching, graphic
130 design . . . the possibilities are endless.

It's not always easy to think about
who you really are and what you
believe in. However, it's the best way to
get to know yourself. And it's the best
135 way to find the job that's right for you.

Source: *100 Great Jobs and How to Find Them* (Fein)
and the Career Services Website (College of Charleston)

AFTER READING

A. MAIN IDEA What is the main idea of the reading? Reread the sentences you highlighted in the reading. Then fill in the correct bubble.

Ⓐ People who love their jobs share certain characteristics.

Ⓑ A person who doesn't like public speaking probably shouldn't be a teacher.

Ⓒ To find a job that is right for you, you must get to know yourself very well.

Ⓓ Self-assessment isn't easy.

B. VOCABULARY CHECK Look back at the reading on pages 26–27. Look for the meanings of these words. The line numbers in the parentheses will help you find the words in the reading. Look for meanings after *be* or *means*. Write the meanings on the lines.

1. self-assessment (Lines 33-34) _____

2. values (Line 41) _____

3. lifestyle (Line 98) _____

4. profile (Line 118) _____

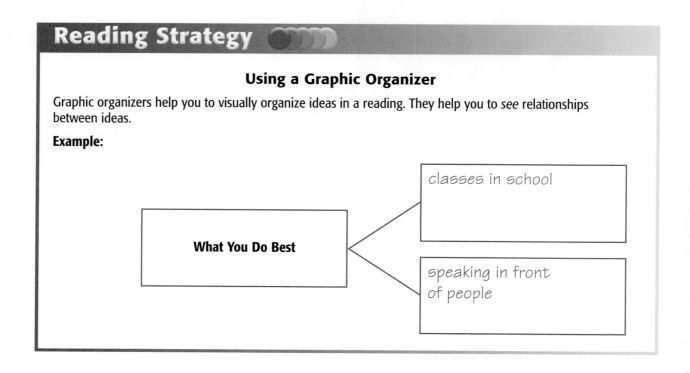

Reading Strategy

Using a Graphic Organizer

Graphic organizers help you to visually organize ideas in a reading. They help you to *see* relationships between ideas.

Example:

What You Do Best → classes in school / speaking in front of people

C. USING A GRAPHIC ORGANIZER The graphic organizer below shows the three parts of self-assessment mentioned in the reading on pages 26–27. Work with a partner. Complete the graphic organizer with some of the examples from the reading.

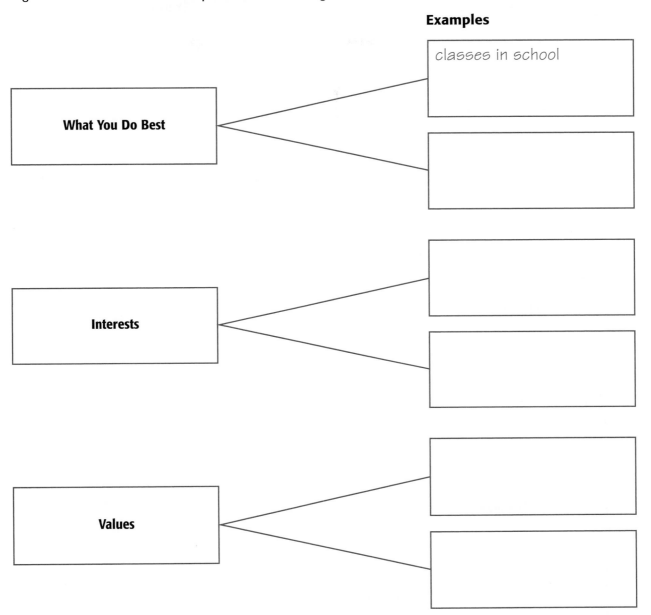

Examples

classes in school

What You Do Best

Interests

Values

D. CRITICAL THINKING Use your knowledge of self-assessment to do your own self-assessment. Provide information about yourself. Complete the graphic organizer with examples.

Examples

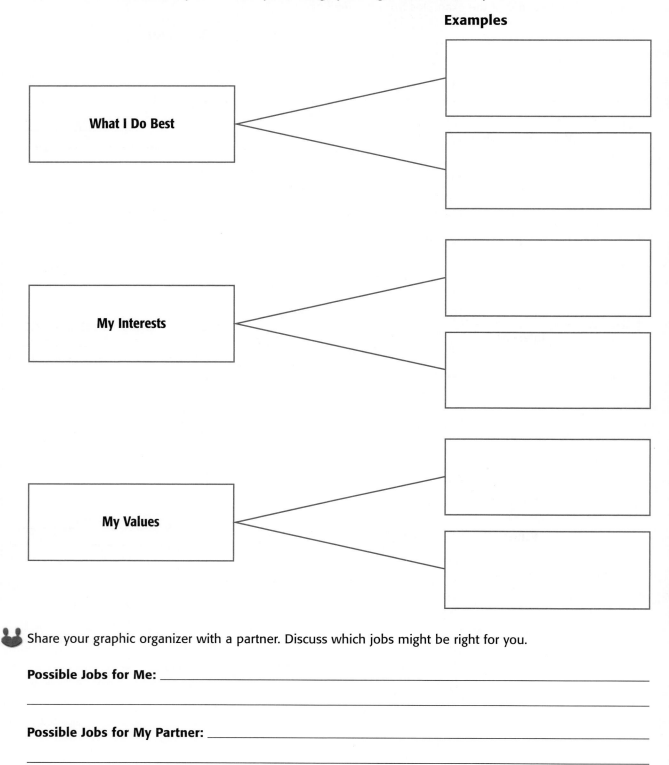

What I Do Best

My Interests

My Values

Share your graphic organizer with a partner. Discuss which jobs might be right for you.

Possible Jobs for Me: _____

_____

Possible Jobs for My Partner: _____

_____

PART 3 ACADEMIC READING
Your Major and Career: Myths and Possibilities

BEFORE READING

A. THINKING AHEAD In small groups, discuss these questions. Some words and phrases from the reading are in red.

1. Do you have a **major**? (A major is your specialization in college.) If yes, what is it? If no, what major might you have in the future?

2. Do you think that your major *must* prepare you for a **career**?

3. Have you talked to **college advisors** or **college career counselors**—people who help you choose a major or prepare for a career? If yes, was it helpful? What did you learn?

4. Look at the career options on page 35. Do any of these careers interest you? How might you prepare for them?

B. VOCABULARY PREPARATION Read the sentences below. The words and phrases in red are from the next reading. First, highlight the definitions that follow *be* or *mean.* Then circle the correct parts of speech for the words and phrases in red. Circle n for *noun* or v for *verb*. See page 5 to review the parts of speech.

	Parts of Speech	
1. *Job-switching* means changing jobs.	n	v
2. **Facilities** are places that provide services.	n	v
3. *Rehabilitation* means treatment to improve a mental or physical problem.	n	v
4. *To be stuck in* something means to be in a situation that you can't get out of.	n	v
5. *To have a head for* something means to be good at something.	n	v
6. A **myth** is an incorrect idea.	n	v
7. *To grow up* means to become an adult.	n	v
8. To **look forward to** is to expect positive events in the future.	n	v

Guessing the Meanings of New Words: Pictures and Captions

You don't always need a dictionary to learn the meanings of new words. Sometimes pictures and captions (the words under the pictures) help you to understand new words. Look at the example on the right.

A water quality specialist tests the water that people drink.

C. GUESSING THE MEANINGS OF NEW WORDS As you read, look for meanings of new words in pictures and captions.

Locating Key Words

For reading comprehension tests, read the questions *before* you read the passage, if possible. Notice key words (words important to the main idea) in the questions. Then look for those key words as you read.

D. LOCATING KEY WORDS Read the sentences in Activity A on page 36. Highlight the key words.

READING

Read about college majors and career choices. As you read, think about this question:
• How do college majors prepare people for careers?

Your Major and Career: Myths and Possibilities

College serves many purposes. It can educate you for a specific career, but it can also offer a more general kind of education. It can expose you to new ideas. It can give you the opportunity to meet new people. It can also help you become more mature. Many people attend college in order to prepare for a
5 career. Others don't have a specific career in mind, but they know that a college degree will help them get some kind of job. However, at some point all college students have to choose a major, and this can be difficult.

Major Myths

After you have chosen a career, you're ready to choose a major. Choosing a major can be stressful. It can seem like a big responsibility. What if you're not sure what you want to do with your life? What if you are interested in a particular major, but your parents want you to study something else? What if you choose a major and then decide you don't like it? Can you change your mind? Also, many students think there is one perfect major for them—that they are good at only one thing.

These are just some of the many myths—incorrect ideas—about choosing a major. Here's what college advisors say about choosing a major:

Myth 1: All of my classes will be in my major, so I don't have to take classes that I don't like.

This is a common belief of students who want to study in the United States. For example, a business major might think, "I don't have to take history or biology because I'm going to major in business." The truth is that in the first two years of college, you have to take "general education requirements." These are classes in a variety of areas such as science, the arts, and English. In the first two years, you will take only a few classes in your major. It's not until your third and fourth years that most classes will be in your major.

Myth 2: When I decide on a major, I will be stuck in that career for the rest of my life.

College career counselors in the United States disagree. First of all, most majors do not lead to one particular career; instead, they give you skills that are useful in many careers. A major in communications is just one example: good speaking and writing skills are necessary in almost any job. A person who majors in communications could become a journalist or a speechwriter or have a career in advertising. In addition, most college graduates combine their academic work with experience, internships (unpaid or low-paying jobs in their field), and further study or training.

More and more people are deciding to change careers after working in a particular career for years. In fact, according to the United States Bureau of Labor Statistics, the average American has 3.5 different careers in his or her life and works for more than 10 employers. In addition, more than 80 percent of American workers have a job that is not directly related to their college major. Job switching is very common in the United States. However, worldwide economic conditions are making career changing more common for people in many countries and cultures.

Myth 3: There is ONE perfect major for me . . . I just need to find it.

No, say college career counselors. There are many career possibilities for most people. First of all, you gain many skills from a college major in addition to learning about your main area of study. For example, all majors will teach

communications, critical-thinking, and decision-making skills. And again, your job choice is largely a combination of your academic work and other skills and
45 interests. Francie Berger is an example. She majored in architecture at Virginia Polytechnic Institute. But Berger combined her major with her love of LEGOs for a career as a toy designer.

Let's take a look at another major as an example: political science. People with this major have many options, depending on their other skills and interests.
50 A political science major with writing skills can work as a newspaper reporter or a speechwriter. A political science major who likes public speaking might find work as a television reporter.

Myth 4: I need to make sure that my parents agree with my career choice.

This is true for some people in the United States. Your parents may be paying for your college education. Also, your parents may believe that it is their
55 job to advise you. This is an important role for parents in many cultures. Most parents want what's best for their children. However, career counselors will remind you of these important facts: You are the one who is going to college. You are preparing for a career. You will be supporting yourself in adulthood. It's important to prepare for a job that *you* will love, one that *you* are good at. It's
60 important to prepare for a job that addresses *your* interests and *your* values and beliefs, not your parents'. Therefore, most college counselors agree that you need to make your own choices about your major.

Career Combos

Can't make up your mind about a major? Still don't know what career is right for you? Try an interesting or unusual combination of fields. Many colleges and
65 universities offer double majors: you can major in *two* subjects. Or you can have a major and a minor. And some students combine their major with further study in another field. Here are some careers that combine two or more fields:

- **Arts Management** Are you interested in the arts but have a head for business? Arts management combines fine arts and business management.
70 Some job titles for people in arts management include general manager of a regional theater, executive director of a chamber music society, and director of a university gallery.

- **Medical Illustration** If you are good at science and love to draw, this field is for you. It combines biology and art. Medical
75 illustrators help communicate medical and scientific information. They are illustrators for medical textbooks, medical advertisements, professional journals, exhibits, and television programs.

A medical illustration

- **Music Therapy** It can be difficult to earn a living as a musician. However, if you like psychology and have a desire to help people, you should think about music therapy as a career
80 choice. Music therapy combines music and psychology. Music therapists use music to help people with physical, psychological,

speech, or hearing problems. They work in many different settings including hospitals, community mental health agencies, rehabilitation centers, day care facilities, nursing homes, and schools.

- **International Business** International business combines business skills with foreign language skills. There are many opportunities in this field because of the growing globalization of business. International business specialists work in their home countries or abroad for exporters, manufacturers, banks, and service companies.

- **Bioinformatics** Bioinformatics is a new and important field. It combines computer science and biology. People trained in bioinformatics use computer technologies to help with medical research. They work for educational institutions, large pharmaceutical (drug) companies, and biotech companies.

Majors and Career Options

Sometimes, majors are directly related to careers. For example, a degree in computer science or engineering might lead directly to a job in those fields. Other majors, such as English or psychology, are not directly related to specific jobs; rather, they can lead to many different careers. This is especially true when people combine these majors with another field, some experience, or further study. Here is a sampling of college majors and the types of careers that they can lead to:

<u>Majors</u>	<u>Career Options</u>
communications ——————————→	news reporter, advertising copywriter, book editor
environmental science ——————→	water quality specialist, environmental lawyer
history and political science —————→	historian, international trade specialist
visual arts ——————————————→	animator, fashion designer, photographer
accounting ——————————————→	certified public accountant, bank manager

---

A book editor

A photographer

A water quality specialist

AFTER READING

A. CHECK YOUR UNDERSTANDING Which sentences are true? Check (✓) the true sentences.

_____ **1.** At U.S. colleges and universities, most classes will be in your major during the first two years.

_____ **2.** Most majors give you skills that are useful in many careers.

_____ **3.** There are several career possibilities with most majors.

_____ **4.** It's very important that students' parents agree with their choice of major.

_____ **5.** It's usually not possible to have two majors.

___✓___ **6.** There are many careers that combine two majors.

B. VOCABULARY CHECK Discuss the jobs below in small groups. What does each person do?

animator	book editor	television reporter
art gallery director	medical illustrator	therapist

Now look back at the reading on pages 32–35 to find three more jobs. Look for words that end in the suffixes *-or* and *-er* (animator), *-ist* (therapist), or *-ian* (politician). Discuss the jobs you find with your group.

C. FINDING IMPORTANT DETAILS With a partner, use the graphic organizer to match some of the majors from the reading with possible jobs.

Majors   **Career Options**

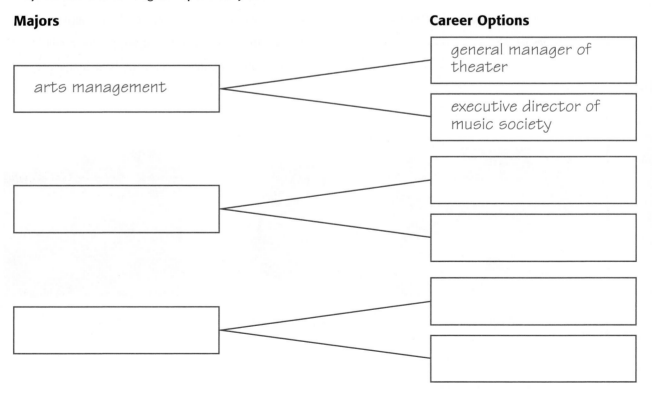

arts management

general manager of theater

executive director of music society

Reading Strategy

Recognizing Words in Phrases: Phrases with Prepositions

Many common phrases contain prepositions. To remember the correct preposition, don't think about the words separately. Memorize the whole phrase.

Example: When I **decide on** a major, I will be stuck **in** a career forever.

D. RECOGNIZING WORDS IN PHRASES: PHRASES WITH PREPOSITIONS Look back at the reading on pages 32–35 to find the phrases in red from the sentences below. The line numbers in parentheses will help you find the phrases. Write the correct prepositions on the lines.

1. A business major might think, "I don't have to take history or biology because I'm going to **major** _____in_____ business." (Line 19)

2. Are you **interested** _____ the arts but have a head for business? (Line 68)

3. People who **are good** _____ math and science might think of engineering. (Line 73)

4. Most majors do not **lead** _____ one particular career. (Line 100)

5. Most American workers have a job that **is** not directly **related** _____ their college major. (Line 104)

E. MAKING CONNECTIONS Combine the information in Part 2 on self-assessment with the information in Part 3 on college majors and careers. Think about what you do best, your interests, and your values to choose the best major for you. Then make a list of five career possibilities for that major. Discuss your list with a partner.

Example: **Major:** English
Career Possibilities: teacher, editor, technical writer, journalist, tour guide

F. WORD JOURNAL Look back at the readings in Parts 1, 2, and 3. Which words are important for *you* to remember? Put them in your Word Journal. (See page 5 to review how to keep a Word Journal.)

G. JOURNAL WRITING Answer this question:
• What is your ideal job? Why?
Write for 10 minutes. Write as much as you can. Don't worry about grammar. Don't use a dictionary.

PART ④ THE MECHANICS OF WRITING

In Part 4, you will practice using the simple present, the present perfect, the simple past, gerunds, and infinitives. You will need this grammar in Part 5 to write a paragraph about yourself.

Simple Present

You use the simple present to talk about repeated actions and general or permanent situations.

Examples: I **work** at a computer company.
James **likes** math and science.

Add an -s for the third person singular *(James, he, she, it)*. For spelling rules for the third person singular with -s, see page 173.

A. SPELLING Follow the spelling rules on page 173. Write the third person singular (-s) forms of the verbs.

1. play _____plays_____
2. take _____
3. study _____
4. fix _____
5. plan _____
6. wish _____

7. dance _____
8. enjoy _____
9. do _____
10. like _____
11. guess _____
12. go _____

B. SIMPLE PRESENT Write the correct forms of the verbs.

James _____lives_____ (live) in Columbus, Ohio. He _____
₁   ₂

(go) to college. He _____ (study) communications at Columbus College. He
                                          ₃

_____ (enjoy) his major and he _____ (hope) to have
          ₄   ₅

a career in hospitality. He _____ (work) hard in school, and he
                                          ₆

_____ (spend) a lot of time on his homework.
          ₇

Present Perfect

You use the present perfect to talk about things that started in the past and continue in the present. To form the present perfect, use *has* or *have* with the past participle (verb + -*ed* or verb + -*en*) of the verb.

Example: James **has lived** in Columbus all his life.

Notice the past participles of these irregular verbs:

go ——→ has/have **gone**   speak ——→ has/have **spoken**

be ——→ has/have **been**   know ——→ has/have **known**

For a list of irregular past participles, see page 175.

Time Expressions with the Present Perfect

You use *since* in a present perfect sentence with time expressions such as *1997, April 3, three o'clock,* and *she was a child.*

You use *for* in a present perfect sentence with time expressions such as *two years, a long time, half an hour,* and *the past five months.*

Examples: Francie has played with LEGOs **since she was three years old**.
James has been a student at the community college **for two years**.

C. PRESENT PERFECT Write the correct forms of the verbs.

James' friend Rafael also wants to work in hospitality. He _____ (live) in
                                                                                    1

Columbus since 2006. He _____ (know) James for two years. He
                                            2

_____ (be) a business major at Anderson College for the last year. He
          3

_____ (work) part-time at the Hinton Hotel since he started school at
          4

Anderson. For the past month, he _____ (go) to see a career counselor
                                                        5

every week, and they _____ (discuss) Rafael's future.
                              6

Simple Past

You use the simple past to talk about things that started and ended in the past. To form the simple past for most verbs, add -*ed* to the present form of the verb: work ——→ worked

Examples: Kim **stayed** at a friend's house after school.
Sharon **lived** in Japan when she was a child.

Irregular verbs do not follow this pattern. Some irregular verbs are the following:

go ——→ went   be ——→ was, were   speak ——→ spoke   take ——→ took

For a list of irregular verbs, see page 175. For a list of spelling rules, see page 173.

D. SIMPLE PAST Write the correct forms of the verbs.

Liana _____ (play) with toy cars when she was a child. She
     ⟨1⟩

always _____ (enjoy) building things. After high school, she
      ⟨2⟩

_____ (go) to Columbus University. At the university, she
⟨3⟩

_____ (take) a lot of science and math classes, and she
⟨4⟩

_____ (major) in industrial design. After college, Liana
⟨5⟩

_____ (become) a car designer.
⟨6⟩

E. REVIEW Write the correct forms of the verbs. Use the simple present, the present perfect, or the simple past.

Dylan _____ (be) a college student. He _____
      ⟨1⟩   ⟨2⟩

(go) to Columbus University for the past two years. Last week, he _____ (see)
                                                                  ⟨3⟩

a career counselor. They _____ (discuss) Dylan's skills, interests, and values.
                         ⟨4⟩

Dylan _____ (have) good communication skills. Since he was a child, he
      ⟨5⟩

_____ (study) music. He _____ (enjoy) foreign
⟨6⟩   ⟨7⟩

cultures and _____ (be) good at foreign languages all his life. In addition, he
             ⟨8⟩

_____ (take) two business classes at Columbus University last semester.
⟨9⟩

F. APPLICATION Write five sentences about yourself. Write about what you do best, your interests, and your values. What classes have you taken in school? What are you good at? What were you interested in as a child? What interests you now? Use simple present, present perfect, simple past, and *for* and *since* in your sentences.

_____

_____

_____

_____

_____

Gerunds and Infinitives

You often use gerunds (verb + *-ing*) and infinitives (*to* + verb) after certain verbs when you talk about careers.

Examples: Tina **enjoys working** in the chemistry lab.
She **hopes to learn** all she can about organic chemistry.

Notice that a gerund follows *enjoy*. An infinitive follows *hope*. Gerunds follow some verbs, and infinitives follow others. Here are just a few of these verbs in each group:

Gerunds follow these verbs:
enjoy   avoid   recommend   suggest   consider

Infinitives follow these verbs:
hope   expect   decide   afford   plan

You can also use a noun after these verbs.

Example: Tina **enjoys movies**.

G. GERUNDS AND INFINITIVES Write a gerund or an infinitive to complete the sentences.

1. If you want to work in a hospital, I recommend _____ (volunteer) in one first.

2. Jim has decided _____ (take) business classes next fall.

3. Tina is taking science classes because she hopes _____ (be) a chemist.

4. Mario can't afford _____ (study) at the university next year.

5. You might consider _____ (work) part-time.

6. Alicia avoids _____ (spend) too much money by taking the bus to school.

PART ⑤ ACADEMIC WRITING

WRITING ASSIGNMENT
In Part 5, you will write a paragraph about your ideal job.

STEP A. CHOOSING A TOPIC Choose a job or career to write about.
• a job that you've hoped for all your life
• a job you just learned about in this chapter
• a cool job
• a job that someone you know has

STEP B. PLANNING YOUR PARAGRAPH Answer the following questions on a piece of paper. Write only short notes, not complete sentences.

1. What is your ideal job? (This will become your topic sentence.)

2. Why is this your ideal job?

3. What are you good at? In other words, what are your skills?

4. What are your interests?

5. What are your values?

Writing Strategy

Determining the Main Idea

A paragraph has one main idea. All of the sentences in the paragraph are about this one main idea. Also, all of the sentences are related to each other. Sentences that are not related to the main idea of the paragraph don't belong.

Example:

> My ideal career is computer game design. This job is ideal for me because it matches my skills, interests, and values perfectly. I loved to play computer games when I was a child. I also enjoyed inventing new games. In high school, I was good at math and science. In addition, I have taken computer programming classes for the past four years. I think that creativity is important, and I like to help people, so I hope to design educational games for children.

STEP C. WRITING THE PARAGRAPH Use your notes from Step B. Write complete sentences in paragraph form. You might make some mistakes, but don't worry about them at this point. Remember:
• The first line of a paragraph is indented.
• All of the other lines go from margin to margin.
• Every sentence begins with a capital letter and ends with a period.
• After a period (.), the next sentence begins on the same line.

STEP D. EDITING Read your paragraph and look for mistakes. Look for:
• paragraph form
• tenses
• gerunds and infinitives
• spelling

STEP E. REWRITING Write your paragraph again, without the mistakes.

CHAPTER 2

The Free Enterprise System

Discuss these questions:
- Look at the picture. Where do you think the people are?
- What product is in the advertisement?
- How does advertising affect what you buy?
- Read the chapter title. What do you think the chapter will be about?

BEFORE READING

A board of directors meeting

A sports equipment store

A bazaar

THINKING AHEAD Look at the pictures above. Discuss these questions with a partner.

1. How are the people in the pictures similar? How are they different?

2. Would you like to work for yourself or for another person? Explain your answer.

3. Can a hobby—a free time activity—become a business? Explain your answer.

4. In your opinion, why are some businesspeople more successful than others?

Read about two businesspeople. As you read, think about the answer to this question:
• How are Yvon Chouinard and Oprah Winfrey similar?

Creative People in Marketing and Business

Yvon Chouinard

When he was a young man, Yvon Chouinard became a rock climber. It was never his idea to turn his hobby into a business, but he didn't like the rock-climbing equipment in stores, so he started to make his own equipment. He used his equipment when he climbed, and soon many of his rock-climbing friends began to buy their equipment from him, too. That was the beginning of his business—Patagonia. Today, Patagonia is a multimillion-dollar company.

Yvon Chouinard rock climbing

Chouinard owns and operates his business, but he works only five or six months each year. What does he do the rest of the time? He *plays*—mountain climbing, skiing, fishing, and surfing. He does what he loves, and while he's climbing (or skiing or fishing or surfing), he gets ideas for new products for his company.

Early in his career, Chouinard became very interested in the environment. When he learned that his climbing equipment was harmful to the environment—the rocks that people were climbing—he created new designs that did not leave a mark on the rocks. However, he does more than this. Patagonia gives 10 percent of its profits to groups that help the environment. In their catalogs, Patagonia also tries to educate the public about ways to protect the environment.

Oprah Winfrey

Oprah Winfrey grew up poor. She learned to read very young. She began her public speaking career at the age of three. At the age of 17, she put these two skills together when she got a job as a news reader on a small radio station. After going to Tennessee State University, she began her career in television.

Today, Oprah—as her many fans call her—is a national talk-show host, a TV producer, and a publisher. With other people, she owns a cable TV channel that targets a female audience. She was the first African-American woman to become a billionaire.

Oprah Winfrey

Clearly, hers is a financial success
75 story. However, she says that her
focus was "never, ever for one
minute" money. She says that she
would do the same work even if she
didn't receive any money for it.
80 According to Oprah, that's how "you
know you are doing the right thing—
because it doesn't feel like work."

Oprah is making a difference in
people's lives. She has worked to
85 end child abuse. She started a book
club on her TV program to
encourage more people to read for
pleasure. And her organization gives
$100,000 to individual people who
90 are using their lives to improve other
people's lives.

AFTER READING

A. CHECK YOUR UNDERSTANDING Write three answers to the question below. Then compare your answers with a partner's answers.

• How are Yvon Chouinard and Oprah Winfrey similar?

1. _Both Chouinard and Winfrey donate some of their money._

2. _____

3. _____

4. _____

B. VOCABULARY EXPANSION *Multi-* is part of a word. It means *many.* With a partner, discuss what the phrases in the box mean.

| multimillion-dollar company | multicultural country | multinational corporation |
| multipurpose room | multiethnic group | |

Critical Thinking Strategy

Making Inferences

Sometimes writers don't state (say) something directly. Instead, readers have to **infer** (guess or figure out) the meaning.

Examples: **You read:** Yvon goes mountain-climbing, skiing, and surfing.
You infer: He enjoys sports. He's energetic and likes challenges.

You read: Oprah began her public speaking career at age three.
You infer: She was a mature child. She is confident and outgoing.

C. MAKING INFERENCES Use your answers in Activity A. In small groups, infer the answer to this question: What is a "secret" to a successful business? In other words, what might be necessary if you want success in business?

How the Market Works—Supply and Demand

BEFORE READING

 A. THINKING AHEAD Look at the picture. Discuss these questions with a partner.

1. Where are these people and what are they doing?

2. What does each person want? What might each person be saying?

3. What will the result of their conversation probably be?

Reading Strategy

Guessing the Meanings of New Words: Using Commas, Dashes, and Parentheses

When you don't know the meaning of a new word, you don't always need to use a dictionary. Sometimes the meaning of the new word (or an explanation of it) is after a comma (,) or dash (–) or in parentheses ( ).

Examples: Jason works for a **corporation**, a business.
Higher prices often make **sellers**—people who sell things—happy.
Ella really likes her **supervisor** (manager).

B. GUESSING THE MEANINGS OF NEW WORDS As you read the next passage, look for the meanings of new words after commas or dashes or in parentheses.

Reading Strategy

Previewing: Having Questions in Mind

In Chapter 1, you learned to connect to a reading topic before you read. One way to do this is to think of one or two questions that you want the reading to answer. Thinking about questions (having questions in mind) as you read helps you to focus and to understand the reading better.

READING

Read about supply and demand. As you read, think about the question below. When you find the answer, highlight it.
• How does the market determine the price of products?

How the Market Works—Supply and Demand

The economic system of countries such as Japan, Canada, Germany, and the United States is **the free enterprise system**—the private enterprise system. This means that the government does not own most businesses. Individuals and groups own them. People are free to produce, buy, and sell what they want. They are free to
5 start a new **enterprise**, a business.

In the free enterprise system, the government does not decide the price of products. The market decides it. But what is "the market"? We know about supermarkets, stock markets, farmers' markets, and meat markets. We can buy and sell things by mail, phone, and computer. These are all part of **the market**—the
10 exchange of goods and services by buyers and sellers.

The market determines the price of products by two general rules: the law of supply and the law of demand. For example, how many tomatoes will people buy at various prices? This is **demand. The law of demand** states that people usually buy more of a product when it's at a lower price. How many tomatoes will the sellers
15 produce at various prices? This is **supply. The law of supply** states that producers will usually supply more of a product if they can increase the price. **Consumers**—people who buy things—want a low price, but producers need to make money. The actions of consumers and producers determine the price.

Let's look at an example. A supermarket has a supply of 600 pounds of tomatoes
20 at $1.99 a pound. After two days, customers have bought only 100 pounds. Soon 600 more pounds are coming to the store. The store manager has a problem—an oversupply of tomatoes. This means she has a **surplus**—too many—so she lowers the price to $1.09 a pound. At this low price, customers soon buy all 500 pounds. This is the **equilibrium price** (the point where supply and demand meet).

25   Another example is the price of gasoline. In 1973, the Oil Producing Export Countries (OPEC) in the Middle East stopped sending oil to Western nations, so in many countries there was a **shortage of**—not enough—gas and oil. Prices went up over 30 percent. In 1979, the supply of oil to the West went down again because of the revolution in Iran, so prices went up again. Consumers and businesses looked for

30   ways to use less gas and oil. They were successful. Demand went down, so prices started to go down. The free enterprise system was working.

Source: *Introduction to Business and Economic World* (Brown and Crow)

AFTER READING

A. MAIN IDEA In the reading, you highlighted the answer to this question: How does the market determine the price of products? Compare your highlighted information with a partner's highlighted information.

B. VOCABULARY CHECK Look back at the reading to find the nine terms below. In the reading, they are in **bold**. Write the definitions on the lines. Don't use a dictionary. The definitions are in the reading.

1. the free enterprise system = _____

2. an enterprise = _____

3. the market = _____

4. the law of demand = _____

5. the law of supply = _____

6. consumers = _____

7. surplus = _____

8. equilibrium price = _____

9. shortage of = _____

C. COMPREHENSION CHECK Look at this chart. What is the equilibrium price of chickens?

The Equilibrium Price of Roasting Chickens			
Supply of Roasting Chickens		Demand for Roasting Chickens	
Quantity	*Price per Pound*	*Quantity*	*Price per Pound*
20 million	$1.25	1 million	$1.25
18 million	$1.15	2 million	$1.15
14 million	$1.05	4 million	$1.05
10 million	95¢	10 million	95¢
8 million	85¢	15 million	85¢
5 million	75¢	25 million	75¢

D. CRITICAL THINKING In small groups, discuss these questions.

1. Why does the price of coffee, strawberries, and computers sometimes go up? Why does the price sometimes go down? (For example, the price of bananas goes up when a hurricane hits Central America.)

2. Look at the two newspaper headlines below. What do you think will happen with supply and demand?

3. Look at this store window. What is probably happening with the laws of supply and demand?

PART ③ ACADEMIC READING Advertising

BEFORE READING

A. THINKING AHEAD In small groups, discuss the questions. The words in red are from the next reading.

1. What are some **trends**—popular activities or fashions—these days? What food, clothing, music, children's toys, and kinds of exercise are people "**into**"—very interested in?

2. What are some companies that produce **designer labels** (clothing produced by famous designers)?

3. What are some **minorities**—small groups within the population—in the United States?

4. Look at the **advertisement** below. What product is it selling? What group of people does the advertisement **appeal to** (try to attract)? Does the advertisement **appeal to** (attract) you?

GOOD DECISION
Purchased GM Certified

BAD DECISION

Buying a GM Certified Used Vehicle is always a good decision. They're from the GM brands you trust. Plus, each one gets a 110+ Point Inspection, a 3-Month/3,000-Mile Comprehensive Limited Warranty, 24-Hour GM Roadside Assistance and a 3-Day/150-Mile Satisfaction Guarantee. To learn more about GM Certified, call 1-888-999-7880 or check out over 80,000 GM Certified Used Vehicles at gmcertified.com.

CHEVROLET   PONTIAC   OLDSMOBILE   BUICK   GMC   THE RIGHT WAY. THE RIGHT CAR.

GM Certified USED VEHICLES

A GM (General Motors) advertisement

B. PARTS OF SPEECH Read the sentences below. The words in red are from the next reading. Circle the correct parts of speech for the words in red. Circle n for *noun*, v for *verb*, or adj for *adjective*.

	Parts of Speech		
1. Sellers of toys often **advertise** during children's TV programs.	n	v	adj
2. Sellers buy **advertising** on radio or TV.	n	v	adj
3. There are **frequent** sales at that store.	n	v	adj
4. More people **frequent** a store that has a lot of sales.	n	v	adj
5. Advertisers **need** to decide on a target.	n	v	adj
6. We learn about people's **needs**, fears, and values.	n	v	adj
7. Advertisers need to decide on a **target**.	n	v	adj
8. They **target** young people who like sports.	n	v	adj

C. VOCABULARY PREPARATION Read the sentences below. The words and phrases in red are from the next reading. In each sentence, find the meaning of the word or phrase in red and highlight it. Do not use a dictionary.

1. **Baby boomers**—the 80 million Americans born between 1946 and 1964—have a lot on their minds these days.

2. Cathy and Jacob hope to have enough money for **retirement** (the time of life when they will stop working, probably after age 65).

3. Madison received an **inheritance** of some money and a house after her parents died.

4. What are some places that young people **frequent**—often visit?

5. I love to go to **spas**, wonderful places for a massage or sauna, but they're expensive.

6. "**Tweens**"—kids ages 8 through 12—are putting away their Barbie dolls in favor of makeup and designer labels.

Reading Strategy

Guessing the Meanings of New Words: *In Other Words*

When you don't know the meaning of a new word, you don't always need to use a dictionary. Sometimes there is a definition or an explanation of the new word after the phrase *in other words*.

Example: This trend is really **hot**–in other words, very recent and popular.

D. GUESSING THE MEANINGS OF NEW WORDS As you read, look for meanings of new words after the phrase *in other words*.

READING

Read about advertising. As you read, think about these questions:
• Why is advertising important? What type of marketing is important these days?

Advertising

Target Marketing

Advertising is an important part of the free enterprise system. This is because different businesses are competing for the same market. They all want customers to buy their product. For this reason, they buy advertising space in newspapers or magazines and advertising time on radio or TV. They
5   hope that advertisements will cause more demand for their product.

Advertisers need to decide on a **target**—in other words, possible buyers for their product. For example, what is the age and sex of their target group? Where do people in their target group live? How much education do they have? What are their political beliefs and values? How much money do they
10 make? What are their interests and needs? Some companies (such as McDonald's) target various groups, so they place **ads**—advertisements—focusing on teenagers, families, and in different languages.

In his book *Market Segmentation*, Art Weinstein explains the importance of **target marketing**—advertising to specific "**market segments**." These
15 "are groups of individuals or organizations with similar characteristics." In the past, companies used **mass marketing**—in other words, the advertising of products to a large, general market. Today, this doesn't work. These days, advertisers need to target very specific groups. However, "in some consumer markets there is a **dual decision-maker**." In other words, two people
20 together decide which product to buy, so it must attract them both. For example, "breakfast cereals must appeal to both the child and the parent."

After advertisers decide on *who* their target is, they then need to determine *where* they should advertise. What is a good place for their ad? Sellers of toys often advertise during children's TV programs. Sellers of expensive clothing
25 advertise in *Vogue* and other fashion magazines.

Advertisers also need to think about people's **motivation**—their reasons for buying something. What makes people buy one product but not another? There are many possible reasons: health, profit, love, entertainment, the need to be part of a group, etc. Clearly, advertisers need to have an understanding
30 of psychology to determine people's motivation.

Today's "Hot Markets"

A study of advertising can also be a study of psychology. When we think about the products that people buy, we learn about their needs, wants, fears, and values. Here is what some
35 experts say about today's hot markets.

Baby boomers—the 80 million Americans born between 1946 and 1964—have a lot on their minds these days. Their kids are going off to college . . . They're worried about
40 retirement. Also, their parents are starting to die. This is leaving some boomers with large amounts of money to manage.

"Hot Market: Boomers," by Chris Penttila, *Entrepreneur*

45

In the United States, minorities are becoming the majority, according to Census Bureau estimates for the next 25 years . . . Multicultural trends are everywhere . . . From music to fashion and beyond, expect the multicultural urban influence to reign supreme [in other words, be very important].

"Multiculturalism," by Nichole L. Torres, *Entrepreneur*

55 The phrase "kids are growing up faster these days" is more true today than *ever* before. Today's teens are frequenting spas and salons, and they're into home decor and remodeling. "Tweens"—kids ages 8 through 12—are decorating their rooms and
60 putting away their Barbie dolls in favor of makeup and designer labels. According to Michael Wood, vice president of Teenage Research Unlimited, a Chicago firm, 12- to 19-year-olds spent $170 billion in 2002 and . . . $176 billion in 2003. "Sports, music,
65 fashion, and technology are the four major areas that consume their attention and time," he says.

"Hot Market: Toddlers/Tweens/Teens," by Chris Penttila, *Entrepreneur*

Sources: "Advertising" (*Scholastic Update*), *Market Segmentation* (Weinstein), "Hot Markets: Toddlers/Tweens/Teens" (Penttila)

AFTER READING

Using Topic Sentences

Most paragraphs have a **topic sentence**. The topic sentence gives the main idea of the paragraph. In many paragraphs, the topic sentence is the first sentence. When you have academic reading (reading for school), highlight the topic sentences as you read. This will help you to focus and understand more.

A. CHECK YOUR UNDERSTANDING Look back at the reading on pages 53–54. Highlight the first sentence of each paragraph. This is the topic sentence. It gives the main idea of the paragraph.

Now write the answers to these questions.

1. Why is advertising important? _____

2. What do advertisers need to **determine** (decide on)? _____

3. What do advertisers need to think about? _____

4. What kind of marketing is important these days? _____

5. What are three "hot" markets these days? _____

B. VOCABULARY CHECK Look back at the reading. Look for a word or phrase in **bold** for each of the definitions below. Write the correct words or phrases on the lines.

1. possible buyers for a product _____ *target* _____

2. advertisements _____

3. advertising to specific market segments _____

4. groups of individuals or organizations with similar characteristics _____

5. the advertising of products to a large, general market _____

6. two people who together decide which product to buy _____

7. reasons for buying something _____

Now, in small groups, compare your answers.

C. WORDS IN PHRASES: PHRASES WITH PREPOSITIONS Look back at the reading on pages 53–54 to find the words and phrases in red from the sentences below. The line numbers in parentheses will help you find the words. Write the correct prepositions on the lines.

1. Different businesses are **competing** ___for___ the same market. (Line 2)

2. They buy advertising space _____ **newspapers or magazines.** (Line 4)

3. They buy advertising time _____ **radio or TV.** (Line 4)

4. Advertisements cause more **demand** _____ a product. (Line 5)

5. Advertisers need to **decide** _____ a target. (Line 6)

6. What is a good **place** _____ their advertisement? (Line 23)

7. They think about people's **reasons** _____ buying something. (Lines 26–27)

8. We **think** _____ the products that people buy. (Line 32)

9. They have a lot _____ **their minds.** (Lines 37–38)

10. They are **worried** _____ retirement. (Line 39)

D. APPLICATION Look at three ads: the two below and the one on page 51. With a partner, fill in the chart on page 57 with information about the ads.

Ads	What is the product?	Who is the target?	Where might you see the ad?	What might be people's motivation to buy this?
Example: Milk ad (page 59)	milk	middle-aged women	women's magazines	They want to be thinner.
GM ad (page 51)				
Kellogg's ad (page 56)				
Tennis ad (page 56)				

E. MAKING CONNECTIONS Look back at the readings in Parts 1 and 2 to answer these questions. Write the answers on the lines.

1. In Part 2, you read about **demand**. What influence does advertising have on demand?

_____

2. In Part 1, you read about the life and work of Yvon Chouinard. What **market segment(s)** does he probably target in his business?

_____

F. WORD JOURNAL Go back to the readings. Which words are important for *you* to remember in Parts 1, 2, and 3? Put them in your Word Journal. (See page 5 to review how to keep a Word Journal.)

G. JOURNAL WRITING Choose *one* of these topics:
- Yvon Chouinard
- Oprah Winfrey
- an ad that you like (or hate)
- the effect of advertising on you

Write about this topic for 10 minutes. Don't worry about grammar. Don't use a dictionary.

PART ④ THE MECHANICS OF WRITING

In Part 4, you will practice using prepositions, the present continuous, the simple present, and adjectives. You will need this grammar in Part 5 to write a paragraph about an advertisement.

Prepositions of Place

Prepositions (or prepositional phrases) can express where something is. Here are some common prepositions of place:

on

in

next to

under

over

between

in front of

in back of / behind

around

Examples: The bee is **on** the box.
The bee is **between** the boxes.
The bee is flying **around** the box.

Here are some prepositional phrases to describe something **on** a page, **in** a picture, or **in** an ad.

in the upper
left-hand corner

at the top

in the upper
right-hand
corner

in the background

in the middle

in the foreground

in the lower
left-hand corner

at the bottom

in the lower
right-hand
corner

Examples: A woman is **next to** the camera.

Her arm is **on** the camera.

A glass of milk is **in** her hand.

The slogan is **in the upper right hand corner** of the ad.

Information is **at the bottom** of the ad.

A. PREPOSITIONS Look at the ad with the tennis players on page 56 and the ad for GM vehicles on page 51. Use them to fill in the blanks below with prepositions and prepositional phrases.

Tennis Ad

1. There are six young people and a dog _____ *on* _____ a tennis court.

2. They are all _____ the net.

3. One tennis player is _____ a wheelchair.

4. The word *Verb* is _____ of the ad.

5. There is information about the players _____ their heads.

GM Ad

6. Three men and their vehicle are _____ a beach at a lake.

7. The lake is _____ of the picture.

8. There are mountains _____ .

9. There is a boat _____ the vehicle.

10. One man is sitting on the vehicle, and another man is _____ it.

11. There is information about the vehicle _____ of the ad.

12. A man and a skunk (a poor choice of a wild animal to feed) are _____ of the ad.

B. PREPOSITIONS Now look at the other ads in this chapter. On a piece of paper, write at least one sentence for each of them. Use a different preposition or prepositional phrase of place in each sentence.

Present Continuous

The present continuous (present tense of *be* + verb + *-ing*) expresses an action that is happening now.

Example: I'm **looking** at an ad for milk.
The car **is stopping** at the traffic light.

Note: For the spelling rules for *-ing* words, see pages 173.

C. SPELLING Follow the spelling rules on page 173. Write the *-ing* form of each verb.

1. stand _____

2. sit _____

3. kiss _____

4. cut _____

5. happen _____

6. wear _____

7. hug _____

8. dance _____

9. lie _____

10. begin _____

11. drop _____

12. fight _____

Stative Verbs

Some verbs, called stative verbs, do not use the present continuous. Stative verbs are sometimes called nonaction verbs. They describe a state or condition, not an action. With stative verbs, use the simple present for an action that is happening now.

Some stative verbs are listed below. A more complete list is on page 176.

believe	know	prefer
belong	like	remember
contain	love	seem
cost	need	understand
hate	own	want

Other verbs have more than one meaning. One meaning is stative. Another is not. Some of these verbs are below. A more complete list is on pages 176–177.

Verb	Stative Meaning	Nonstative Meaning
	(Do not use the present continuous.)	(Use the present continuous for an action that is happening now.)
have	own Pam **has** a new car.	eat, drink; experience He**'s having** lunch. They**'re having** fun.
look	seem Mike **looks** happy.	use one's eyes I**'m looking** at a magazine.
see	use the eyes; understand I **see** them over there. Yes, I **see**. I know what you mean.	meet with; visit He**'s seeing** the doctor now.
guess	suppose I **guess** they're rich.	make an estimate I don't know. I**'m** just **guessing**.
think	believe; have an opinion I **think** they're happy.	use one's mind, consider What **are** you **thinking** about?

D. STATIVE VERBS The paragraph below is about the ad on page 59. Write the correct form of the verbs: present continuous or simple present.

A woman _____ (stand) next to a camera. I _____
            1   2

(think) she might be an actress, but I _____ (not remember) her name.
                                     3

She _____ (look) happy. She _____ (smile)
       4   5

and _____ (wear) a "milk mustache." She _____
       6   7

(have) a glass of milk in her right hand, and she _____ (rest) her arm
                                                  8

on the camera. The glass _____ (seem) to have a narrow "waist," so I
                         9

_____ (guess) the idea is that drinking milk can keep a person slim.
10

E. STATIVE VERBS Look again at the ad on page 51 and the two ads on page 56. On a separate piece of paper, write 10 sentences about them. Use the present continuous or simple present.

Using Adjectives

Adjectives describe something or someone. Adjectives can come before nouns.

Examples: There's a **huge** dog.
          Jude is a **strong** man.

Adjectives can also come after verbs such as *be*, *look* (= seem), or *seem*.

Examples: The little girl is **cute**.
          Roger seems **nice**.
          The snake looks **dangerous**.

Note: Adjectives in English are never plural.

Using Multiple Adjectives

Sometimes you want to use two adjectives with one noun. Different kinds of adjectives must be used in a specific order. The order is *opinion, size, condition, age, color, nationality*.

Example: Gina wore a **new white** dress. (*Age* comes before *color*.)
          It's an **expensive new** watch. (*Condition* comes before *age*.)
          Scott bought a **big expensive** car. (*Size* comes before *condition*.)

F. USING ADJECTIVES Write 7 sentences about one or more of the ads in this chapter. Use two or more adjectives in each sentence.

_____

_____

_____

_____

_____

_____

Test-Taking Strategy

Finding Grammatical Errors

Many standardized English tests have a grammar or writing section. Often, there are sentences with four underlined words or phrases. One of them is incorrect. You need to find and identify the error. One way to find the error is to read the sentence quickly. If you pause or stop while reading, you may have found the error. Your mind may be pausing because the sentence doesn't look right.

G. FINDING THE ERRORS Circle the letter under the word or phrase that is incorrect.

1. In the ad, there <u>is</u> a woman with a glass of milk <u>in</u> her hand, which
              A   B

   <u>is resting</u> on a camera, and the slogan is <u>on the upper right-hand corner</u>.
     C   D

2. <u>Do you see</u> that <u>foolish young</u> man (<u>next</u> the tree) who <u>is trying</u> to feed a skunk?
      A   B   C   D

3. Two <u>young attractive</u> people <u>are walking</u> <u>on</u> a beach <u>in the middle</u> of this picture.
         A   B   C   D

4. There <u>is</u> some wonderful food <u>on</u> the table <u>in front of</u> two women who <u>have</u> brunch.
        A   B   C   D

PART ⑤ ACADEMIC WRITING

WRITING ASSIGNMENT

In Part 5, you will write a paragraph of description about an ad.

STEP A. CHOOSING A TOPIC Choose *one* ad to write about.
- one of the ads from this chapter
- another ad (one with a clear target) that you find in a magazine

STEP B. PLANNING YOUR PARAGRAPH Answer the following questions on a separate piece of paper. Write only short notes.

1. What is the product in the ad and who is the target of this ad? (This answer will become your topic sentence.)

2. What is happening in the ad?

3. Describe the scene. (Use adjectives and prepositions of place.)

Writing Strategy

Organizing a Paragraph of Description

A paragraph has one topic. The topic sentence is the first sentence. It includes the topic and main idea of the paragraph. The other sentences give details—more information—about the main idea. In a paragraph:

- the first line is indented

- all of the other lines go from margin to margin

- every sentence begins with a capital letter and ends with a period

- after a period (.), the next sentence begins on the same line

In a paragraph of *description*, the adjectives are important. Choose them carefully, and put them in the correct order. Also, use prepositions of place to describe where everything is.

Example:

Middle-aged women are the target for this milk ad. In this ad, a confident, dark-haired woman is standing next to a camera. Her right arm is resting on the camera. She's holding a glass of milk. She's smiling, and there's a milk mustache on her upper lip. The slogan ("Got milk?") is in the upper right-hand corner of the ad, and there's information at the bottom.

STEP C. WRITING THE PARAGRAPH Use your notes from Step B. Write complete sentences in paragraph form. You might make some mistakes, but don't worry about them at this point.

STEP D. EDITING Read your paragraph and look for mistakes. Look for:
- paragraph form
- prepositions of place
- tenses
- stative verbs
- spelling
- the order of adjectives

STEP E. REWRITING Write your paragraph again, without the mistakes.

UNIT ① VOCABULARY WORKSHOP

Review vocabulary that you learned in Chapters 1 and 2.

A. MATCHING Match the definitions to the words. Write the correct letters on the lines.

__*a*__	**1.** goods	**a.** products to sell
_____	**2.** values	**b.** too much of something
_____	**3.** lifestyle	**c.** small parts of a population
_____	**4.** major	**d.** a way of living life
_____	**5.** minorities	**e.** things that are important to your life
_____	**6.** motivation	**f.** one's main area of study at college
_____	**7.** myth	**g.** popular activities or fashions
_____	**8.** rehabilitation	**h.** treatment to improve a problem
_____	**9.** surplus	**i.** an incorrect idea
_____	**10.** trends	**j.** reasons for doing something

B. TRUE OR FALSE? Which sentences are true? Which are false? Fill in Ⓣ for *True* or Ⓕ for *False*.

1. An **animator** is a kind of politician. Ⓣ **Ⓕ**

2. A **college career counselor** helps you choose a major or prepare for a career. Ⓣ Ⓕ

3. A **consumer** is someone who buys something. Ⓣ Ⓕ

4. **Job-switching** means keeping one job for life. Ⓣ Ⓕ

5. People who are between the ages of 13 and 18 are **tweens**. Ⓣ Ⓕ

6. **Market segments** are groups of individuals or organizations with similar characteristics. Ⓣ Ⓕ

7. A **shortage** is too much of something. Ⓣ Ⓕ

8. **Medical illustrators** communicate medical or scientific information. Ⓣ Ⓕ

C. PHRASES WITH PREPOSITIONS Which prepositions can you put together with the words in red? Write the correct prepositions on the lines. You may use each preposition more than once.

about	at	for	in	on

1. Chris is going to **major** _____ in _____ accounting because he likes math.

2. Frannie **excels** _____ art, so she's going to become a graphic designer.

3. It's hard to **decide** _____ a major because there are so many choices!

4. Advertisers need to **think** _____ people's reasons for buying things.

5. Because of good advertising, there is now more **demand** _____ the company's product.

6. Rick is **interested** _____ computers. He's used them since he was a child.

7. Sam is **good** _____ languages, so he's going to major in Spanish.

8. Some baby boomers are **worried** _____ retirement.

D. FREQUENTLY USED WORDS Some of the most common words in English are in the box below. They are among the most frequently used 500-1,000 words. Fill in the blanks with words from the box. When you finish, check your answers on page 21.

child	friendship	met	remembered	worked
every	get	played	today	years

Anthony Marinaccio operates the Cyclone Roller Coaster at the Coney Island amusement park in New York. Marinaccio grew up on Coney Island. As a _____, he

_____ at the beach and rode the amusement park rides
2

_____ day. As a teenager, he _____ at the park and
3   4

did many different jobs. _____, Marinaccio greets and seats roller coaster
5

riders. How did he _____ the job? Luck and _____
6   7

played a part. One day, over 25 _____ ago, when he didn't have a job, he
8

_____ his childhood friend, Gerald Menditto, on the street. Menditto is the
9

Cyclone's operations manager, and he _____ that Marinaccio was a hard
10

worker with a good sense of humor (he likes to laugh).

BIOLOGY

Chapter 3
Animal Behavior

Chapter 4
Nutrition

CHAPTER 3

Animal Behavior

Discuss these questions:
- Look at the picture. What animals are in the picture?
- Do you think the animals are fighting or playing? Explain your answer.
- How are animals and humans the same? How are they different?
- Read the chapter title. What do you think the chapter will be about?

BEFORE READING

👥 **THINKING AHEAD** Look at the pictures. Discuss these questions with a partner.

1. What kinds of animals do you see? What are their names in English? In what parts of the world do you think these animals live?

2. What is happening in each picture?

3. In your opinion, which of these actions did the animals learn to do? Which actions did the animals do instinctively—without learning?

READING

Read about two unusual animals. As you read, think about these questions:
• What did the octopus learn?
• Why is the tiger unusual?

Animal Tales

Octopus Intelligence

With its eight powerful arms, an octopus can swim backwards or pull itself over rocks on the ocean floor. An octopus is very strong, but is it intelligent? People at the
5 Hellabrunn Zoo, in Germany, might have an opinion about this.

An octopus

Glass jars do not exist in the ocean, the natural environment of an octopus, so you might not expect an octopus to know how to
10 open one. However, at the Hellabrunn Zoo, an octopus named Frieda had the motivation to learn how to open a jar. The motivation was food. Frieda watched her human keepers as they opened glass jars with food inside. From watching them, she learned how to twist off the lid and reach inside for the food.

Interestingly, she will not open just *any* jar. She doesn't open jars that contain fish.
15 According to a representative of the zoo, "She'll open only jars containing her favorite foods, such as shrimp, clams, and crabs."

Brother Tiger

How much of an animal's behavior is from nature (biology)? How much is from nurture (life experience)? Can nurture change an animal's nature? Can early life
20 experience have an influence on an adult animal?

You might think that for a hungry tiger, a baby pig would naturally be lunch. However, for Saimai, a two-year-old Bengal tiger, piglets are not lunch. According to *Best Friends Magazine,* Saimai plays with them as if they
25 were his brothers. That's because when he was a cub, Saimai grew up with piglets. He thought that *their* mother was *his* mother. She suckled him—fed him milk—while she was suckling her real babies.

Will this behavior continue or will Saimai suddenly
30 return to his instinctive nature? Nobody knows the answer, but maybe those piglets shouldn't get *too* close to their "brother," just in case.

Source: *Best Friends Magazine*

Saimai

AFTER READING

A. CHECK YOUR UNDERSTANDING In small groups, discuss these questions.

1. What did the octopus learn to do?

2. Why doesn't the tiger eat the pigs?

B. VOCABULARY EXPANSION Look back at the reading to find words with these meanings. Write the words on the lines.

1. What word means "baby pigs"? _____

2. What word means "baby tiger"? _____

Reading Strategy

Understanding Punctuation: Quotation Marks and Italics

Writers use quotation marks ("...") for different reasons. One reason is to state a person's exact words.

Example: "Give me the ball," Jim said.

Writers also use quotation marks when the word in quotation marks really means something different.

Example: The child picked up her "baby."
(It wasn't really a baby. It was her doll.)

Writers also use *italics* for different reasons. One reason writers use italics is for the title of a newspaper, magazine, or book.

Example: The story appeared in **Best Friends Magazine**.

Writers also use italics for stress (emphasis).

Example: She will not open just **any** jar.

Writers also use italics to mean "the word . . ."

Example: **Cub** means "baby tiger."

C. UNDERSTANDING PUNCTUATION Discuss these questions with a partner.

1. In the section of the reading about the octopus, circle the quotation marks. What is the reason for the quotation marks?

2. In the section about the tiger, underline examples of words in italics. Circle the quotation marks. What are the reasons for this punctuation?

BEFORE READING

A. THINKING AHEAD Look at the pictures above. In small groups, discuss these questions.

1. What animals do you see?

2. What is happening in each picture?

3. Do you or does someone you know have a pet, such as a dog or cat? How does the pet communicate with people? Does the pet understand people? If so, how do you know?

4. What do you know about animal communication? (How do animals communicate?)

B. VOCABULARY PREPARATION Read the sentences below. The words in red are from the next reading. Find the meanings of the words in red and highlight them. Do not use a dictionary.

1. One kind of African monkey has three **calls** (sounds) to other monkeys in the group.

2. Each call is **distinct**—specific and different from the others.

3. In Africa, **apes** (gorillas and chimpanzees) communicate in many of the same ways that humans do.

4. They use body movements, **gestures**—movements with their hands—and calls.

5. They learned verbs such as *throw, touch,* and *fetch* (go and get).

Previewing for the Topic: Headings

It's a good idea to look over a reading quickly before you read it. This will help you think about the topic when you read. One way to preview a reading is to look at the headings (the **bold** section titles on the left). Another way is to look for important new vocabulary in **bold** print.

C. PREVIEWING FOR THE TOPIC Look over the reading, "Animal Communication" on pages 74–76. What are the five headings? Write the headings on the lines below.

_____   _____

_____   _____

_____

Reading Strategy

Guessing the Meanings of New Words: *That Is*

When you don't know the meaning of a new word, you don't always need to use a dictionary. Sometimes there is a definition or an explanation after the phrase *that is*. It might define or explain one word, a phrase, or an idea. *That is* means "in other words."

Example: Children who can't hear learn American Sign Language–**that is,** a system of hand signals.

D. GUESSING THE MEANINGS OF NEW WORDS As you read, look for meanings of new words after the phrase *that is*.

READING

Read about animal communication. As you read, don't use a dictionary. Try to guess the meanings of new words. Think about these questions:
• What are some ways that animals communicate?
• Can animals use language?

Animal Communication

Ways that Animals Communicate

Animals communicate with each other in different ways. Some insects such as ants use smell to tell other ants, "There's food over there." Bees (another type of insect) communicate with special movements. They do a kind of dance to tell other bees the location of flowers. Many mammals, such as elephants and whales, exchange information by sound. A humpback whale can hear another whale 745 miles (1,200 kilometers) away!

Humans

We humans use language—that is, a system of symbols to represent ideas. There are thousands of languages. In each one, words symbolize ideas and there are grammar rules. Most languages are spoken, but some languages are not. For example, American Sign Language (ASL) is a language of hand gestures, or signs. Many people wonder, "Can animals learn language, too? Can humans and animals communicate with each other?"

Monkeys and Apes in the Wild

In the wild (that is, in a natural environment), monkeys and apes have several ways to communicate. One kind of African monkey has three calls (sounds) to communicate with other monkeys in the group. Each call is distinct—specific and different from the others—and communicates a specific kind of danger. The monkeys use a different call for each of the three animals that prey on (that is, hunt) monkeys. In Africa, apes (gorillas and chimpanzees) communicate

A chimpanzee in the wild

in many of the same ways that humans do. They use body movements, gestures—movements with their hands—and calls. One group of chimps in the forest of East Africa has twenty-five distinct calls.

Apes in Captivity

In the 1960s and 1970s, Beatrix and R. Allen Gardner, two professors at the University of Nevada, taught American Sign Language to young chimpanzees in captivity—that is, a human environment. They named their first chimp Washoe. By the age of five, Washoe knew and used more than 160 signs. With these words, she communicated with humans. She also signed to herself, her doll, and other animals. Washoe and the other chimps often put signs together to make a new word. For example, "metal hot" was a cigarette lighter. "Smell fruits" were oranges and lemons. "Drink fruit" was watermelon.

Since 1972, Penny Patterson, then a graduate student at Stanford University in California, has taught ASL to a gorilla named Koko. Koko uses over 500 signs to express her

Koko, a gorilla, and Patterson, a human

needs and wants. Like Washoe, she
sometimes creates new words. Once,
she didn't know the word *ring*, so
she called it a "finger bracelet."
When a human asks her, "Who are
85 you?" she answers, "Fine gorilla
animal." She also tells jokes and
sometimes lies.

Dolphins in Captivity

For many scientists, the goal is to
answer this question: Can animals
90 understand *syntax*—that is, the
grammar rules of word order? Louis
Herman of the University of Hawaii
decided to study dolphins—very
intelligent ocean mammals.
95 Herman's strategy was to teach a
language of arm signals to one
dolphin and a language of sounds to
another.

The dolphins learned nouns such
100 as *ball* and *hoop*. They learned verbs
such as *throw, touch,* and *fetch* (go
and get). They learned to follow a
two-word command—for example,
"Fetch ball." They learned
105 prepositions (*in, on, under*) and
words of direction (*left* and *right*).

Dolphin learning syntax

Herman found the answer to the
question: yes, dolphins *can*
understand some syntax. For
110 example, they can learn the
difference between direct and indirect
objects—take *the ball* (direct object)
to *the hoop* (indirect object). Now
the question is, how much more is
115 possible?

Source: *Biology: The Dynamics of Life* (Biggs, Hagins,
Kapicka, Lundgren, Rillero, Tallman, Zike, and the
National Geographic Society)

AFTER READING

A. CHECK YOUR UNDERSTANDING Write your answers to these questions on a separate piece of
paper. Then compare your answers with a partner's answers.

1. What are seven kinds of communication mentioned in the reading?

2. Which examples in the reading show that some animals can create (make) their own words?

3. Which example shows that some animals can understand grammar?

B. VOCABULARY CHECK Look back at the reading on pages 73–75. Look for the phrase *that is*. Write the words or phrases for these definitions on the lines.

1. a system of symbols to represent ideas (Lines 14–16) _____

2. a natural environment (Lines 28–29) _____

3. hunt (Lines 44–45) _____

4. a human environment (Lines 61–62) _____

5. the grammar rules of word order (Lines 90–91) _____

Reading Strategy

Classifying

Classifying means putting similar things in groups. As you read, try to classify new information, either on a piece of paper or in your head. Classifying will help you to focus and to understand a reading better.

C. CLASSIFYING In small groups, classify the animals in the box into different types. Write the animals in the chart below.

~~ant~~	chimp	duck	gorilla	pigeon	tuna
bee	cockroach	eagle	human	salmon	shark
cat	dog	elephant	monkey	termite	vulture
chicken	dolphin	goose	pig	tiger	whale

Fish	Insects	Mammals	Birds
	ant		

PART ③ ACADEMIC READING How Do Animals Learn?

BEFORE READING

A. PREVIEWING Before you read the passage on pages 79–80, quickly look it over. Look at the headings for six types of learned behavior. Write them on the lines.

_____   _____

_____   _____

_____   _____

B. VOCABULARY PREPARATION Read the sentences below. The words in red are from the next reading. Find and highlight the meaning of the word in red in each sentence. Then circle the correct parts of speech for the words in red.

	Parts of Speech

1. **Behavior** is the way that animals act.   n   v   adj

2. A **jackdaw**—a kind of bird—learns to build a nest.   n   v   adj

3. This is a way of learning by **association**—that is, putting together   n   v   adj
   different ideas.

4. Dogs **salivate** (produce liquid in the mouth) when they smell food.   n   v   adj

5. Learning allows an animal to be **adaptable**—that is, able to change in a   n   v   adj
   new situation.

Reading Strategy

Guessing the Meanings of New Words: *Such As* and *For Example*

Sometimes examples can help you to guess a new word or idea. You can find examples after the phrases *such as* and *for example*.

Example: Dolphins can understand some syntax. **For example**, they can learn the difference between direct and indirect objects.

C. GUESSING THE MEANINGS OF NEW WORDS As you read, notice examples that help you to understand new ideas.

Read about animal behavior. As you read, highlight the topic sentence—the first sentence—in each paragraph. Think about this question:
• How do animals learn?

How Do Animals Learn?

Behavior is the way that animals act. For example, how do they get food or take care of their young? How do they find a place to live or protect themselves from danger? Behavior is either **innate** or **learned**.

Innate Behavior

Much behavior is **innate**; that is, animals are *born* with it. Their genes
5 determine the animals' behavior. In other words, the behavior is a biological inheritance. Some innate behaviors are simple, such as a **reflex** or a **fight-or-flight response**. What happens if something suddenly passes in front of your eyes? You blink—that is, you quickly close and open your eyes. This is a reflex. You have no control over it. Think about
10 a time when you were very afraid. Your heart began to beat faster, and you began to breathe faster. Maybe your body started to shake. You were having a fight-or-flight response. Your body was preparing for
15 danger. You had no control over this behavior. Both a reflex and a fight-or-flight response are simple and quick.

Territoriality: Male sea lions fight for territory

Another, more complex, kind of innate behavior is **instinct**. Two kinds of
20 instinctive behavior are **territoriality** and **migration**. Many animals have a strong sense of territory—a place that they "own." For example, a male sea lion protects his area of beach by attacking
25 other male sea lions that come onto it. This is territoriality. Another instinctive behavior, migration, is the movement of animals from one part of the world to another. For example, every fall, many
30 birds fly from North America to South America because there is more food in South America during the winter. They migrate back north in the spring. Whales also migrate seasonally.

Migration: Geese fly south for the winter

Habituation

One simple type of *learned* behavior is **habituation**. This happens when an animal learns to feel comfortable in a new situation and doesn't pay attention to it anymore. For example, young horses are often afraid of noisy streets. But after a while, they learn to pay no attention to the normal sights and sounds of a city.

Imprinting

Another kind of learned behavior is **imprinting**. Some animals (such as ducks, geese, and other birds) do not innately know how to recognize other members of their own species (group). They learn this in the first day or two of life. For example, imagine a mother duck in a lake. Four or five small ducklings are swimming after her. They know to follow her. Ducklings quickly imprint on the first moving thing that they see. Usually this is their mother, but not always.

Trial and Error

In **trial-and-error** learning, an animal tries to do something many times before it is successful. This is how a human learns to ride a bicycle. She probably has to fall off many times before she can ride successfully. A jackdaw—a kind of bird—learns to build a nest in this way, too. At first, it uses almost *anything* in its nest: leaves, grass, stones, pieces of glass, or empty cans. With experience, it learns that leaves and grass make a more comfortable nest than stones or glass. Of course, this learning happens faster if there is **motivation** such as hunger or a need for comfort.

Association

One way of learning by **association**—that is, putting together different ideas—is **conditioning**. In 1900, Ivan Pavlov, a Russian biologist, studied conditioning in dogs. Dogs innately salivate (produce liquid in the mouth) when they smell food. Pavlov rang a bell *every* time he gave the dog food. Soon the dog started to associate the *sound* of the bell with the *smell* of food. After some time, it salivated when it heard a bell alone, without food. Another form of association is **observation**—that is, watching another animal do something. Many kinds of young birds and mammals observe their parents and learn what to eat and how to eat it, for example.

Insight

The most difficult, complex type of learning is **insight**. With insight, an animal uses past experience to solve a new problem. We humans use insight, for example, when we work on a new math problem.

Learning is important for all animals in a new environment. It allows an animal to be adaptable—that is, able to change in a new situation.

Source: *Biology: The Dynamics of Life* (Biggs, Hagins, Kapicka, Lundgren, Rillero, Tallman, Zike, and the National Geographic Society)

AFTER READING

A. VOCABULARY CHECK Match the types of behavior on the left with the correct definitions on the right. Write the correct letters on the lines.

_____ **1.** association

_____ **2.** habituation

_____ **3.** imprinting

_____ **4.** innate behavior

_____ **5.** insight

_____ **6.** trial and error

a. learning from past experiences

b. not learned behavior; animals are born with it

c. recognizing one's own species

d. feeling comfortable in a new situation

e. putting together different ideas

f. doing something many times and finally succeeding

B. VOCABULARY EXPANSION Look back at the reading on pages 79–80. Write the words or phrases for the definitions on the lines.

1. quickly close and open your eyes (Line 8): _____

2. in the winter, spring, summer, or fall (Line 34): _____

3. a bird's home (Line 48): _____

4. something similar to water (Line 55): _____

5. people (Line 63): _____

6. able to change in a new situation (Line 66): _____

C. MAIN IDEA AND DETAILS A graphic organizer like the tree diagram below is one way to classify things and to show the connections between them. Fill in the tree diagram with information from the reading.

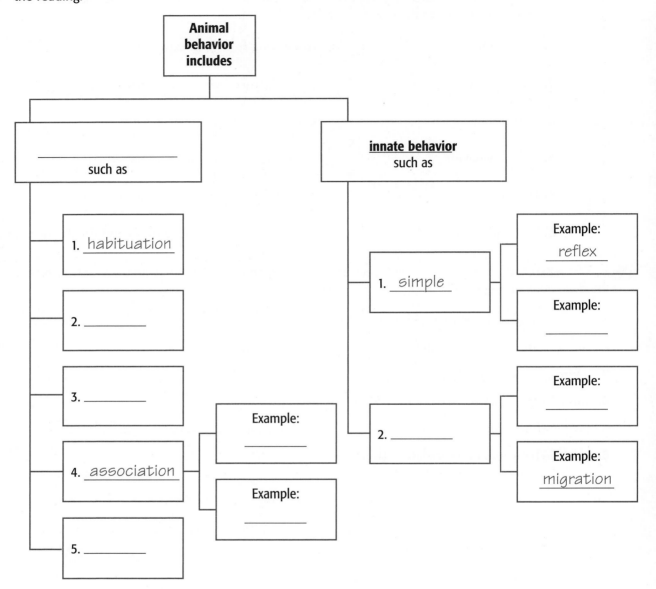

Animal behavior includes

_____ such as

1. habituation

2. _____

3. _____

4. association

Example: _____

Example: _____

5. _____

innate behavior such as

1. simple

Example: reflex

Example: _____

2. _____

Example: _____

Example: migration

Understanding Pronouns

On many standardized tests, you need to show that you understand pronouns (such as *he, she, it,* and *they*). Every pronoun refers to a noun or noun phrase before it. To find the correct noun for a pronoun, follow these steps.

1. Decide if the pronoun is plural (such as *they*) or singular (such as *it*). Also, decide if it is masculine (*he*) or feminine (*she*).

2. Look to the left of (and maybe above) the pronoun. Look at both the same sentence and the sentences before it.

3. Find a noun to fit the pronoun. For example, look for a singular, masculine noun to fit the pronoun *he*.

Example: Behavior is the way that (animals) act. How do **they** get food or take care of their young?

D. PRONOUNS There is a pronoun in red in each sentence below. Fill in the correct bubble for the noun or noun phrase the pronoun refers to.

1. Much behavior in the animal world is innate. That is, an animal is born with **it**; it is the animal's biological inheritance.

   Ⓐ behavior   Ⓑ animal world   Ⓒ animal   Ⓓ inheritance

2. Habituation occurs when an animal learns to feel comfortable in a new situation and doesn't pay attention to **it** anymore.

   Ⓐ habituation   Ⓑ animal   Ⓒ a new situation   Ⓓ attention

3. Some animals (such as ducks, geese, and other birds) do not innately know how to recognize other members of their own species (group). **They** learn this in the first day or two of life.

   Ⓐ some animals   Ⓑ ducks   Ⓒ other members   Ⓓ species

4. Learning is important for any animal in a new environment. **It** allows an animal to be adaptable—that is, able to change in a new situation.

   Ⓐ learning   Ⓑ animal   Ⓒ environment   Ⓓ situation

Critical Thinking Strategy

Applying Information

Applying information is an important critical thinking skill. To *apply* information is to use information that you already know in a new situation. This will help you to understand the information. Also, it is proof that you really understand. Professors will often ask you to apply information to new situations on exams or in essays.

Example: You read: At first, Laura's cat did not like Laura's new dog, but later the cat just ignored the dog.
          You think: This is an example of habituation.

E. APPLICATION Below are four examples of learned behavior. Review the types of behavior in your tree diagram on page 82. Write the correct types of learned behavior on the lines.

Konrad Lorenz and baby geese

A chimp figures out how to reach bananas.

1. In the 1930s, the biologist Konrad Lorenz studied geese. He took care of their eggs. When the baby geese hatched (were born), Lorenz was the first moving thing that they saw. In a day or two, they learned to follow him everywhere.

This is an example of _____.

2. You move to a house on the beach. At first, you can't fall asleep at night. The sound of the ocean waves keeps you awake. After a week, you fall asleep easily. You don't notice the waves anymore.

This is an example of _____.

3. You feed your new cat canned cat food. You open the can with an electric can opener. At first, your cat smells the food and then begins to *meow*. After a few weeks, she runs to the kitchen and *meows* as soon as she hears the can opener.

This is an example of _____.

4. A chimp found a way to reach bananas that were too high for him. First, he tried to reach the bananas by jumping. Next, he tried to throw a box at the bananas. Finally, he put boxes on top of each other and climbed up. Soon the bananas were within reach.

This is an example of _____.

F. MAKING CONNECTIONS Look back at the readings in this chapter to answer these questions. Write the answers on the lines.

1. In Part 1, you read about an octopus and a tiger. What type of learning did the octopus use to open the jar? Why did the tiger think that he was a pig? (In other words, what kind of learning was going on?)

_____

2. In Part 2, you read about communication. What are several kinds of behavior that humans use to learn language?

_____

G. EXPANSION Interview three classmates about a learned behavior. First, think about your answer to the question in the chart. Then ask three classmates the question. Write their answers in the chart.

Classmate	Question What is an example of *habituation, trial-and-error, association,* or *insight* (choose one) from your life?

H. WORD JOURNAL Go back to the readings in Parts 1, 2, and 3. Which words are important for *you* to remember? Put them in your Word Journal.

I. JOURNAL WRITING Choose *one* of these topics:
• an animal that surprised or interested you from these readings
• something that you are having problems learning
• your favorite animal

Write about this topic for 10 minutes. Don't worry about grammar. Don't use a dictionary.

PART ④ THE MECHANICS OF WRITING

In Part 4, you will practice using the simple past, transition words, objects, and articles. You will need this grammar in Part 5 to write a paragraph about something that you have learned.

Simple Past

The simple past expresses something that happened—started and ended—in the past. There are two forms of the simple past: regular and irregular.

Most verbs are regular. Just add -ed to the simple form of the verb.

Examples: The octopus **watched** the humans. (watch + *ed* = watched)
　　　　　She **learned** how to open glass jars. (learn + *ed* = learned)

Irregular verbs do not follow this pattern.

Examples: The tiger **thought** he was a pig. (think ⟶ thought)
　　　　　He **grew up** with pigs. (grow up ⟶ grew up)

To form the negative of both regular and irregular verbs, use *did* + *not* (or the contraction *didn't*) + the simple form of the verb.

Example: The tiger **didn't attack** his "brother" pigs.

A list of irregular verbs is on page 175. Spelling rules for words with -ed are on page 174.

A. SIMPLE PAST Write the simple past of the verbs in parentheses.

When I _____ (be) a child, my family _____
　　　　　　　　1　　　　　　　　　　　　　　　　　　　　　　2

(have) a cat called Teddy. He _____ (be) very sweet and friendly. Then one
　　　　　　　　　　　　　　3

day, I _____ (find) a lost cat and _____ (bring) her
　　　　4　　　　　　　　　　　　　　　　　　　5

home. We _____ (name) her Little Bit. She _____
　　　　　　6　　　　　　　　　　　　　　　　　　　7

(make) herself at home and _____ (seem) comfortable from the
　　　　　　　　　　　　8

beginning. Unfortunately, Teddy _____ (not like) her at all. He
　　　　　　　　　　　　　　9

usually _____ (hide) from her, but sometimes he
　　　　　10

_____ (attack) her. Slowly, over the next few months, he
　　11

_____ (get) used to her, and they _____
　　12　　　　　　　　　　　　　　　　　　13

(become) friends.

Combining Ideas

And

You can join two or more nouns, verbs, adjectives, or clauses with the word *and*. Notice the use of *and* in these examples.

Examples:
He understands **and** speaks the language. (two verbs)
Animals communicate by sight **and** sound. (two nouns)
Animals communicate by sight, sound, **and** smell. (three nouns; two commas)
The Gardners were studying animal communication, **and** they taught ASL to a chimpanzee. (two clauses; comma)
The Gardners were studying animal communication **and** taught ASL to a chimpanzee. (one clause before *and;* no subject after *and;* no comma)

When and *Because*

You can join two clauses with *when* or *because*. Don't use a comma when *when* or *because* are in the middle of a sentence.

Examples: Our cat was unhappy **when** we brought a new cat home.
We worried **because** the cats weren't getting along well.

Time

When you write about actions in order of time, you might need to use time words or phrases. Here are some of them.

first   at first   after a while   then   later on   finally

Examples: They wanted to teach language to dolphins. **First,** they taught several nouns to the dolphins. **Later on,** they taught them verbs. **Then** they gave the dolphins simple commands.

Note: You can begin a sentence with these time words. Use a comma after each transition word (except for *then*).

B. COMBINING IDEAS Combine these ideas. Use the word in parentheses to join sentences or begin a new sentence.

1. She tells jokes. Sometimes she tells lies. (and)

   Example: She tells jokes, and she sometimes tells lies.

   _____

2. The dolphins learned nouns. The dolphins learned verbs. The dolphins learned prepositions. (and)

   _____

   _____

3. The chimp was able to reach the bananas. He found a way to use boxes as a ladder. (when)

   _____

   _____

4. The dolphin carefully watched the arm signals. She swam over to the ball. (then)

_____

_____

5. The octopus watched the humans. She figured out how to open the jars herself. (after a while)

_____

_____

6. The chimp signed to herself. The chimp signed to her doll. The chimp signed to other animals.

_____

_____

Using Direct and Indirect Objects

There is a direct object (D.O.) immediately after some verbs. A direct object is a noun or noun phrase. If you look at the verb and ask "What?", you will find the direct object.

Example: The dolphin watched **the man**.
                verb   **D.O.**

       (The dolphin watched what? _The man_)

If the verb is transitive, it must have an object. Some transitive verbs are _enjoy, like, give, take, bring,_ and _find_. (Your dictionary shows that a verb is transitive with the letters _vt._ or _tran_.)

Examples: ~~The dolphin takes.~~ (incorrect)
            The dolphin takes **the ball**. (correct)

Some verbs also have an indirect object (I.O.). When you use an indirect object, you express _to whom_ (or _to what_) you give, take, bring (etc.) something. There are two possible positions for an indirect object–after the direct object and between the verb and the direct object.

Examples: The dolphin took **the ball** to **her**.
              verb   **D.O.**   **I.O.**

            The dolphin took **her the ball**.
              verb **I.O.**   **D.O.**

Note: Do not use _to_ if the indirect object comes immediately after the verb.

C. DIRECT AND INDIRECT OBJECTS Write each sentence in a different way. Change the order of the two objects and add or remove _to_.

1. Brad gave some food to the dog.

   Brad gave the dog some food. _____

2. Bring me the ball.

_____

3. Patterson has taught ASL to Koko.

_____

4. Betty's strategy was to teach arm signals to the dolphins.

_____

5. Lance gave the cat some food.

_____

6. Jen taught a young chimp American Sign Language.

_____

Using Articles: *A, An,* and *The*

There are many rules for articles. One is to use *a* or *an* for the first time you mention a count noun and *the* for each time after that. A count noun is one that can have a plural form.

Examples: One day **a** woman found **a** seagull. **The** seagull seemed to have **a** broken wing. **The** bird dragged **the** wing slowly along the sand.

There is an exception to this rule. If both the writer and reader know which noun the writer means, the writer uses *the* even for the first mention.

Example: Every morning I get up at 7:00 and go into **the** kitchen. I pour water into **the** coffee maker. (Which kitchen? The kitchen in my house. Which coffee maker? My coffee maker.)

D. USING ARTICLES Fill in the blanks with *a, an,* or *the*. Use the rules in the box above.

In _____ ocean off _____ California coast, _____ sea otter swims down to _____ ocean
       1   2   3   4

floor. _____ otter picks up _____ clam (its dinner) and _____ rock. It swims back up to _____
       5   6   7   8

surface of _____ water. Then _____ otter lies on its back and uses its stomach as _____ table. It
           9   10   11

uses _____ rock as _____ tool to open _____ clam.
     12   13   14

E. REVIEW/EDITING Read the paragraph below. There are at least six mistakes in it. They are mistakes with the simple past tense, objects, articles, transition words, and the punctuation of transition words. Find and correct them.

    Forty-five years ago, ~~the~~ *a* young anthropologist went to Gombe, in Tanzania, to study chimpanzees

in the wild. Her name was Jane Goodall. At first, she didn't got close to the chimps, because they were

afraid of her. Later on they begin to feel comfortable around her and she was able to learn surprising

things about them. For example, she learned that wild chimps create tools, make war.

PART 5 ACADEMIC WRITING

WRITING ASSIGNMENT

In Part 5, you will write a paragraph about a learned behavior. It can be something learned through habituation, trial and error, association, or insight.

STEP A. CHOOSING A TOPIC Choose a learned behavior and the type of learning that was involved.

(You can use your tree diagram on page 82 to help you choose a topic.) Choose *one* from:
• your own life   • a classmate's life
• your pet's life   • a classmate's pet's life

What was the type of learning?
• habituation   • association
• trial and error   • insight

STEP B. PLANNING YOUR PARAGRAPH Answer the following questions on a separate piece of paper. Write only short notes.

1. What was the learned behavior, and what was the type of learning? (This will become your topic sentence.)

2. Write a list of the steps in learning this behavior. Put the steps in chronological order—the order of time.

3. For new words, use a dictionary or ask someone—another student or your teacher.

Organizing a Paragraph of Process

In a paragraph of process, you write about each step in a series of actions. It's important to write these in order of time. (What happens first? What happens next?) For this assignment, begin with the topic (your learned action) in the first sentence. After this, write each step from your plan in a complete sentence.

Example:

I learned to like *kimchee* by habituation. *Kimchee* is a pickled vegetable (usually cabbage), and it has a very strong taste. I first experienced this dish when I went to live in Korea for a few years. At first, I hated it because it smelled of garlic. But the smell was everywhere—in every restaurant and home. People ate it at almost every meal. I couldn't avoid having it on the table in front of me. After a while, the smell didn't seem so strange. Then one day I took a small bite. I didn't like it much, but it wasn't terrible. Every day, I ate a little more. Finally, I was able to eat a lot of it, and I learned to enjoy it.

Notice the following in the example:
- the use of transition words
- the use of the simple past tense

Analysis: Look for transition words in the example paragraph. Highlight each one. Notice the punctuation.

STEP C. WRITING THE PARAGRAPH Use your notes from Step B. Write complete sentences in paragraph form. You might make some mistakes, but don't worry about them at this point.

STEP D. EDITING Read your paragraph and look for mistakes. Look for:
- paragraph form (indentation, margins)
- the topic sentence
- the order of the steps
- the simple past tense
- the use of articles
- transition words and punctuation for them

STEP E. REWRITING Write your paragraph again, without the mistakes.

CHAPTER 4

Nutrition

Discuss these questions:
- Look at the picture. What is the man eating?
- How is this food good for his health?
- Do most people think about what is in the food that they eat? Do you?
- Read the chapter title. What do you think the chapter will be about?

PART ① INTRODUCTION McDonald's Around the World

BEFORE READING

A fast-food meal

A vegetarian dish

THINKING AHEAD Look at the pictures. Answer these questions with a partner.

1. Do you eat at fast-food restaurants? Why or why not?

2. Do you eat meat or are you a vegetarian—someone who does not eat meat?

3. In your opinion, what kinds of food are healthy—good for your health? What kinds of food are unhealthy?

4. What is your favorite food? Why?

Read about fast food. As you read, think about this question:
• How does McDonald's **adapt to** (try to match) the food preferences of different cultures?

McDonald's Around the World

Many companies want to do business around the world. To be successful, these companies must adapt to local cultures. This is especially true for food
5 companies. One example is McDonald's. McDonald's adapts to local cultures. In other words, it matches local food preferences. For example, McDonald's offers *ayran* (a popular chilled yogurt
10 drink) in Turkey, McLaks (a grilled salmon sandwich) in Norway, and teriyaki burgers in Japan. In New Delhi, India, Hindus do not eat beef, and Muslims do not eat pork. There, the
15 burgers are made of mutton (sheep meat) and called "Maharaja Macs."

And if you're vegetarian, as many strict Hindus are, there's the McAloo Tikki burger. This is a spicy vegetarian
20 burger made of potatoes and peas. There's also a vegetarian mayonnaise that's made without eggs. (As any cook knows, this is very difficult to do!)

Sandip Maithal, the manager of
25 McDonald's in New Delhi says, "Cooking lamb (young sheep meat) is very different from beef. There's less fat. And we have two different groups of people to cook the vegetarian and
30 nonvegetarian food. Workers with green aprons make only the vegetarian food. Workers with black aprons make the nonvegetarian food."

"We have even separated the two
35 menus," says Maithal. "We know that in India, vegetarians don't even want to have to read about meat dishes."

Around the world, McDonald's is quickly becoming a *local* restaurant, not
40 a foreign import (something that is sent from another country). The menus contain food items that match the local customs. In addition, the workers are all local people. If you go to a McDonald's
45 anywhere in the world—in India, Brazil, or Manila—you will probably buy your burger from a person who lives nearby and who speaks the local language.

Perhaps McDonald's has found a
50 way for people with very different tastes and customs to all eat together.

Source: *Globalization* (Zwingle)

A McDonald's in India

AFTER READING

A. MAIN IDEA Discuss this question with a partner:

• How does McDonald's try to adapt to the food preferences of different cultures?

B. FINDING DETAILS Use information in the reading to match the food preferences to the countries. Write the correct letters on the lines.

_____ **1.** mutton   **a.** India

_____ **2.** salmon   **b.** Norway

_____ **3.** teriyaki   **c.** Turkey

_____ **4.** yogurt   **d.** Japan

Reading Strategy

Understanding Italics

As you learned in Chapter 3, writers use italics for different reasons. One reason writers use italics is for foreign words.

Example: Many French dishes use a *bordelaise* sauce.

Writers also use italics to stress important words, such as words that don't show opposite ideas.

Example: Jason doesn't like Chinese food, but he *loves* Korean food.

C. UNDERSTANDING ITALICS Look back at the reading on page 95. Find words in italics to answer the questions below. Write the answers on the lines.

1. What is the name for a popular chilled yogurt drink in Turkey? _____

2. What is the opposite of something that is foreign? _____

Critical Thinking Strategy

Forming an Opinion

As you read, try to form your own opinion about the ideas in a passage. When you form an opinion, have reasons to support it. This helps you to focus on and to remember important information.

Example: While reading the passage on page 95 you think, "McDonald's seems like a smart company because it thinks about the local market."

D. FORMING AN OPINION Discuss these questions with a partner:

- Is McDonald's a good or bad example of American culture? Does it have a good or bad influence on other cultures? That is, does it cause changes that are good or bad? Give reasons for your opinion.

PART ② GENERAL INTEREST READING
Eating Bugs Is Only Natural

BEFORE READING

 **A. THINKING AHEAD** In small groups, discuss these questions.

1. What foods seem strange to you?

2. What foods will you *not* eat? Why?

3. Have you ever eaten bugs (insects)? If no, *would* you eat an insect? Why or why not?

B. VOCABULARY PREPARATION Read the sentences below. The words in red are from the next reading. Find the meanings of the words and highlight them. Do not use a dictionary.

1. Gene DeFoliart is a professor of **entomology** (the study of insects).

2. Roman **aristocrats**—that is, wealthy people—ate insects.

3. In South Africa, some people eat insects with cornmeal **porridge**, a grain dish.

4. Eating insects is practically **taboo** (not allowed) in Europe and North America.

5. Some people in Japan enjoy **aquatic** insects, insects that live in water.

6. One hundred pounds (45 kg.) of **feed**—animal food—produces 10 pounds (4.5 kg.) of beef.

7. There is also the problem of **pesticides**. Pesticides are poisons that kill insects.

8. Ten thousand years ago, people ate bugs to **survive**—that is, to stay alive.

9. Eating insects is an old **tradition** (custom).

10. In Mexico, many people consider agave worms to be **culinary** insects—good to cook and eat.

Reading Strategy

Previewing: Reading the Introduction

One way to preview a passage is to carefully read the introduction (the first paragraph). The introduction will usually state the topic and the main idea. This will help you to know what to expect from the rest of the reading.

C. READING THE INTRODUCTION Read just the first paragraph of the passage. Then discuss these questions with a partner.

1. What is the topic?

2. What kind of information will the reading probably have?

D. USING PICTURES AND CAPTIONS Before you read, look at the pictures and captions—words under the pictures. Which bugs do you know? Which bugs are new to you?

READING

Read about eating bugs. As you read, think about the questions below. When you find the answers, highlight them.
• Who eats bugs?
• Are bugs a healthy food?

Eating Bugs Is Only Natural

Do you eat bugs? No? Then you may be different from many people around the world. Throughout history, people have enjoyed insects as food. In fact, many cultures still do.

Ten thousand years ago, hunters and gatherers ate bugs to survive—that is, to stay
5 alive. They probably learned to eat bugs by watching animals. Animals ate bugs, and this showed people which bugs were safe, according to Gene DeFoliart, a professor of entomology (the study of insects) at the University of Wisconsin-Madison.

10 Eating insects is an old tradition (custom). The ancient Romans and Greeks dined on insects. Pliny, the first-century Roman scholar and author of *Historia Naturalis,* wrote about eating insects. He wrote that Roman
15 aristocrats—wealthy people—loved to eat beetle larvae (the young form of an insect). Aristotle, the fourth-century Greek philosopher and scientist, wrote about eating cicadas. He wrote that cicada larvae were delicious.

20 The Bible encouraged people to eat locusts, beetles, and grasshoppers. According to Biblical stories, one man survived in the desert because he ate locusts. In the 1800s in America, Paiute (Native-American) women hunted the wingless Mormon cricket. They used them in a high-protein bread.

A grasshopper

Insect Cuisine

Many types of insects appear on menus today. Bugs are a traditional food in many cultures in Africa, Asia, and Latin America, DeFoliart says. In Ghana during the spring rains, people collect winged termites (insects that eat wood). They fry, roast, or use them in bread. In South Africa, some people eat termites in a grain dish. In China, beekeepers eat bee larvae. They believe that the larvae keeps them strong.

Some people in Japan enjoy aquatic insects, insects living in water. They are cooked in sugar and soy sauce. Dragonflies are boiled in coconut milk with ginger and garlic in Bali.

A tarantula

New Guineans and aboriginal Australians enjoy grubs. In Latin America, people use cicadas, tarantulas, and ants in some traditional dishes. In Mexico, many people enjoy one of the most famous culinary insects, the agave worm. They cook agave worms and eat them on tortillas. They also put them in bottles of mescal, an alcoholic drink.

Cultural Choices

However, eating insects is still unusual in the United States and Europe. In fact, it's practically taboo (not allowed). One reason, DeFoliart, the Wisconsin entomologist, said, is that a long time ago, Europeans started to grow plants for food. Insects destroy food crops, so they became the enemy instead of food.

Manfred Kroger, a professor emeritus of food science at Penn State University in Pennsylvania, says the food that people choose to eat is cultural. For example, many Westerners regularly eat shrimp, lobster, pork, and oysters—foods that other cultures do not eat.

A dragonfly

Environmentally Friendly Protein

Kroger and DeFoliart believe that insects are very healthy. Hamburger, for example, is about 18 percent protein and 18 percent fat. A cooked grasshopper, however, is almost 60 percent protein and is only about 6 percent fat. In addition, like fish, the fatty acids in insects are unsaturated and therefore healthier.

65   DeFoliart also believes that eating insects is economical and good for the environment. According to DeFoliart, insect farming is much more economical than cattle production. That is, it costs less. One hundred pounds (45 kilograms) of feed—animal food—produces 10 pounds (4.5 kilograms) of beef. The same amount of feed produces 45 pounds (20 kilograms) of crickets.

70   There is also the problem of pesticides. Pesticides are poisons that kill insects. DeFoliart points out that people are poisoning the planet by killing insects with pesticides. Instead, we could eat insects and keep these dangerous pesticides away from the plants that we eat.

Source: *For Most People, Eating Bugs Is Only Natural* (Guynup and Ruggia)

AFTER READING

A. CHECK YOUR UNDERSTANDING Write your answers to the following questions on the lines. Then compare your answers with a partner's answers.

1. Who ate bugs in the past? Who eats bugs today?

_____

2. The entomologists—DeFoliart and Kroger—give three reasons that people should eat bugs. What are they?

_____

_____

B. MAKING INFERENCES Think about what you read in the passage. In small groups, discuss these questions:
• What is protein? Is it a good thing? Does it make bugs a healthy food?
• What are fatty acids? Are they good for you? What kind of fatty acid is best?
• *In general*, what are locusts, beetles, crickets, grubs, and cicadas?

C. VOCABULARY EXPANSION Look back at the reading. Find one word that means *eaten* and one expression that means *ate*. Write them on the lines.

1. a word (Line 2) _____

2. an expression (Line 11) _____

D. MAKING CONNECTIONS How might McDonald's adapt to a culture that eats bugs? With a partner, create (think of) a McDonald's dish with insects for the following cultures:
• Mexican
• aboriginal Australian
• South African

BEFORE READING

A. THINKING AHEAD In the chart below, write 10 of your favorite foods in the left column.

Favorite Foods	Healthy?	Why?
1. _baked chicken_	☑ yes ☐ no	_good protein_
2. _____	☐ yes ☐ no	_____
3. _____	☐ yes ☐ no	_____
4. _____	☐ yes ☐ no	_____
5. _____	☐ yes ☐ no	_____
6. _____	☐ yes ☐ no	_____
7. _____	☐ yes ☐ no	_____
8. _____	☐ yes ☐ no	_____
9. _____	☐ yes ☐ no	_____
10. _____	☐ yes ☐ no	_____

With a partner, decide if each food in your chart is healthy or not. Check (✓) *yes* or *no*. Then write why the food is healthy or not. If you are not sure, guess.

Reading Strategy

Previewing: Figures and Tables

Textbooks often have many figures and tables. Figures are pictures; tables are lists of information in categories. Previewing—or looking quickly at—the figures, tables, and captions before you read will help you understand the main ideas of the reading.

B. USING FIGURES AND TABLES Before you read, scan (quickly look at) the reading. Find the following figures and tables.

- Figure 4.1
- Figure 4.2
- Figure 4.3
- Table 4.1
- Table 4.2

Now answer the following questions. Use the figures and tables. Fill in the correct bubbles.

1. What is the topic of this reading?

   (A) animals   (B) food   (C) medicine

2. Look at Figure 4.2. What foods are good sources of protein, fat, and carbohydrates?

   (A) oil and butter   (B) candy   (C) fruits, vegetables, grains, and dairy products

3. Look at Figure 4.3. Which nutrient is probably the most important?

   (A) fat   (B) carbohydrate   (C) fiber

4. Look at Tables 4.1 and 4.2. What do they tell you about vitamins and minerals?

   (A) the foods they are in   (B) how your body uses them   (C) A and B

Reading Strategy

Guessing the Meanings of New Words: Using Examples

When you don't know the meaning of a new word, you don't always need to use a dictionary. Sometimes you can guess the meaning of a new word by finding examples of it. The examples are often in the same sentence, right next to the word. Sometimes examples of the new word come after the expression *for instance*.

Example: Many people eat **dairy products**–for instance, cheese and yogurt–every day.

Examples of new words also sometimes come before the words *and other*.

Example: You don't need to eat a lot of butter, oil and other **fats**.
(Fats = foods such as butter and oil.)

C. GUESSING THE MEANINGS OF NEW WORDS As you read, look for explanations of new words in examples. Look for words before *and other* and after *for instance*.

Read about **nutrition**—how the body uses food. As you read, think about the questions below. When you find the answers, highlight them.
• What are the six nutrients in food? What does each nutrient do in the body?

Nutrition Basics

Everyone should know a little bit about nutrition—how food does or doesn't make you healthy. Knowing about nutrition can help you make healthy food choices. **Nutrients** are the chemicals in food. There are six different nutrients: proteins, fats, carbohydrates, vitamins, minerals, and water.

Proteins, Fats, and Carbohydrates

5   **Proteins** are nutrients that build and repair the body. Large parts of tissues—for instance, bone, muscle, and skin—come from protein. Foods such as chicken and other
10 meats, eggs, fish, and nuts, supply protein.

Fats are nutrients that supply your body with energy. Fats contain large
15 amounts of energy. Salad dressing, butter, and cooking oils are foods high in fat.

Carbohydrates are
20 nutrients that also supply you with energy. What then is the difference between fats and carbohydrates? The body
25 uses carbohydrates first for energy. The body stores fats; that is, it keeps them for later. Then, if necessary, it uses the fats for energy. Foods that contain starches and sugars (for instance, bread and fruit) supply carbohydrates.

30 A person can remain healthy only if he or she gets the correct amounts of each nutrient. You should not get more or less of a nutrient than your body can use. What's the best way to stay healthy? Eat foods with the correct amount of each nutrient. A good daily diet is 55 to 65 percent carbohydrates, less than 30 percent fats, and 10 to 15 percent protein.

Figure 4.1: There are six nutrients—chemicals—in food.

Figure 4.2: These foods are excellent sources of protein, fat, and carbohydrates.

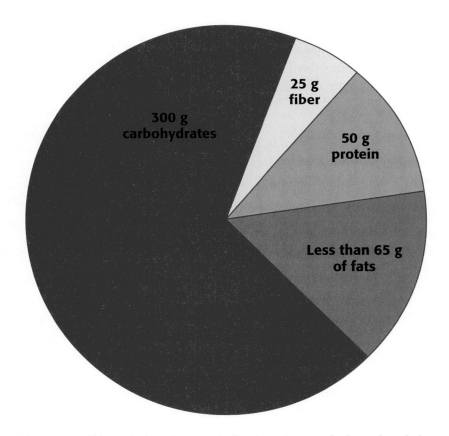

Figure 4.3: This graph shows how much of each nutrient your body needs each day.

Vitamins

35   **Vitamins** are special chemicals that are necessary in many different body processes. You need vitamins in small amounts every day. If you get too much or not enough of a vitamin, you can get sick. For example, if you take too much vitamin A, you can lose your hair or have liver problems.

Vitamin	How Used in Body	Problems if Not Enough	Foods	RDA
A (retinol)	vision, healthy skin	night blindness, rough skin	liver, broccoli, carrots	5000 IU
B_1 (thiamine)	allows cells to use carbohydrates	digestive problems, muscle paralysis	ham, eggs, raisins	1.5 mg
B_2 (riboflavin)	allows cells to use carbohydrates and proteins	eye problems, cracking skin	milk, yeast, eggs	1.7 mg
B_3 (niacin)	allows cells to carry out respiration	mental problems, skin rash, diarrhea	peanuts, tuna, chicken	20.0 mg
C (ascorbic acid)	healthy membranes, wound healing	sore mouth and bleeding gums, bruises	green peppers, oranges, lemons, tomatoes	60.0 mg
D (calciferol)	bone growth	bowed legs, poor teeth	egg yolk, shrimp, milk, yeast	400 IU

Table 4.1: Vitamins

40   When you read a food label, you will see the vitamins listed as A, B_1, B_2, B_3, C, and D. Sometimes you see their chemical names, for instance, ascorbic acid (vitamin C) or retinol (vitamin A). Look at Table 4.1 for the names of the vitamins you need each day.

    Notice the column marked RDA in Table 4.1. RDA means "recommended dietary allowance." It is the amount of each vitamin and mineral that a person 50 needs each day to stay healthy. Some amounts for vitamins are in IUs— international units; others are in mg—milligrams. Both are very small measurements. You can find RDA percentages for the vitamins and minerals on many food labels.

Minerals

Minerals, like vitamins, are chemicals. You also need them in very small amounts. Some of the minerals your body needs are iron, calcium, magnesium, 55 and sodium. Table 4.2 lists these minerals and how your body uses them. You can get sick if you don't get enough minerals. For example, your teeth and bones can become weak if you don't get enough calcium.

Mineral	How Used in Body	Problems if Not Enough	Foods	RDA
Iron	helps form blood cells, helps blood carry oxygen	anemia, feeling tired	liver, egg yolk, peas, enriched cereals, whole grains	15 mg
Calcium	helps form bones and teeth	bones and teeth become weak or brittle	milk, cheese, sardines, nuts, whole-grain cereals	1 g
Magnesium	helps form bones and teeth	muscles twitch	potatoes, fruits, whole-grain cereals	325 mg
Iodine	helps make thyroid gland chemical	causes thyroid gland to enlarge	seafood, eggs, milk, iodized table salt	150 μg*
Sodium	muscle contractions, nerve messages	dizziness, tired feeling, cramps	bacon, butter, table salt	1200 mg

*μg = microgram (one microgram is 1/1,000,000 of a gram)

Table 4.2: Minerals

Water

Water is also an important nutrient. It cools your body. You can see this happen when you sweat. Also, many chemicals in the body can combine only 60 with water. Therefore, many chemical changes can happen only with water. Finally, water helps to carry away body wastes. The average adult needs two liters (8.5 cups) of water a day.

Source: *Biology: An Everyday Experience* (Kaskel, Hummer and Daniel)

AFTER READING

A. MAIN IDEA What are the six nutrients in food? With a partner, use the information that you highlighted to help you find the answer. Write the nutrients on the lines.

_____   _____

_____   _____

_____   _____

B. FINDING DETAILS Complete the graphic organizer below with information about the nutrients in food. Why does the body need them? What foods have them? Give two examples of each.

Nutrients: Why the Body Needs Them   **Examples**

Proteins:
to build and repair body parts   meats

Fats:

Carbohydrates:

Vitamins:

Minerals:

C. VOCABULARY CHECK Match the nutrition terms in the box with their meanings. Write the words in the chart below.

ascorbic acid	IU	protein	tissue
carbohydrates	mg	retinol	vitamins
fat	~~nutrients~~		

Meanings	Nutrition Terms
chemicals your body needs, such as vitamins	nutrients
nutrients that build and repair body parts	
bone, muscle, and skin	
nutrients that supply your body with energy (two words)	
chemicals that help body tissue grow and repair	
another name for vitamin C	
another name for vitamin A	
an abbreviation for international units	
an abbreviation for milligrams	

D. USING YOUR KNOWLEDGE Look again at your chart on page 101. Were you correct about which foods were healthy? Make changes in the chart if necessary.

E. WORD JOURNAL Go back to the readings in Parts 1, 2, and 3. Which words are important for *you* to remember? Put them in your Word Journal.

F. JOURNAL WRITING Choose one of these topics:
• What is your favorite food and why?
• What do you usually eat? In other words, what is your typical diet?
Write for 10 minutes. Don't worry about grammar. Don't use a dictionary.

PART ④ THE MECHANICS OF WRITING

In Part 4, you will practice using count and noncount food nouns, quantity expressions, and cause and effect expressions. You will need this grammar in Part 5 to write a paragraph about your diet.

Count and Noncount Food Nouns

Some food words are count nouns. That is, you can count them. You can use *a* or *an* with them. Count nouns have singular and plural forms. For the plural form, you add -*s* to the end of the word.

Singular	Plural
a hamburger	hamburgers
an egg	eggs

Examples: I ate **an egg**.
              singular

      David ate a lot of **eggs**.
                   plural

Other food nouns are noncount nouns. You cannot count noncount nouns. You cannot use *a* or *an* with them. They do not have a plural form. For example: rice, bread.

Examples: I ate **rice**.
      David ate a lot of **rice**.

Some Count and Noncount Food Nouns

Count		Noncount	
dairy product	pea	bread*	yogurt
hamburger	apple	fruit*	vitamin C, A, D, etc.
nut	egg	tea*	butter
potato	vegetable	rice	lamb
sandwich	dish	cheese*	wine*
bean	meal	mutton	fish
vitamin	taste	beef	food*
chili pepper	doughnut	coffee*	milk

* Some noncount foods (*tea, coffee, cheese*) are countable when you are talking about varieties (types) or numbers of servings.

Examples: French **cheeses** include brie and camembert.

      We ordered two **coffees**.

Vitamin is countable, but a particular vitamin—for example, *vitamin C*—is not.

Example: I take **vitamins** every day. **Vitamin C** helps wounds to heal.

A. COUNT AND NONCOUNT FOOD NOUNS
Is the word in red in each sentence below a count noun or noncount noun? Circle the correct answer.

1. Harry had salmon **sandwiches** for lunch.   (Count)   Noncount

2. I buy **bread** at Fred's because it tastes best.   Count   Noncount

3. Fresh **vegetables** are good for you.   Count   Noncount

4. Chili peppers have a lot of **vitamins**.   Count   Noncount

5. Many people in the world drink **tea**.   Count   Noncount

6. Do apples have **vitamin C**?   Count   Noncount

B. TALKING ABOUT FOOD
Work with a partner. Follow the example below. With count nouns use *a/an* and the singular form or a number and the plural form. With noncount nouns, use *some*. Use the food words from the "Count and Noncount Food Nouns" box on page 109 or your own words.

Example: **A:** What did you have for dinner last night?
            B: I had some fish. What did you have?
            A: I had a hamburger.

Too Much and Too Many

When you talk about nutrition, you often talk about quantities—the total amount or number. When you are talking about a large quantity, you can use *too much* or *too many*.

Use *too many* with count nouns.

Example: I ate **too many doughnuts**. I feel terrible.
            (*Doughnuts* is a count noun.)

Use *too much* with noncount nouns.

Example: I ate **too much butter**. I got sick.
            (*Butter* is a noncount noun.)

Note: *Too* means "more than enough," usually in a bad way.

C. *TOO MUCH* AND *TOO MANY*
Look at the word in red in each sentence. Is it a count or a noncount noun? Write *too much* or *too many* on the lines.

1. David ate _____ **oysters** last night.

2. James drank _____ **coffee** this morning.

3. Kate took _____ **vitamin A**.

4. Bill ate _____ **chili peppers**.

5. Rafael ate _____ **hamburgers** at lunch.

A Lot Of and Not Enough

You can also talk about a large quantity with the expression *a lot of*. You can use *a lot of* with both count and noncount nouns.

Examples: I had **a lot of** vegetables for dinner.
I put **a lot of** milk in my coffee.

When you talk about a small amount of food, you can use the expression *not . . . enough* in a negative way. You can use it with both count and noncount nouns.

Examples: I do **not** take **enough** vitamins.
Sue does **not** eat **enough** protein.

D. *A LOT OF* AND *NOT ENOUGH* Write sentences with these cues on the lines. Use *a lot of* or *not enough*. Use the correct form of *do* in negative statements. Use the simple present.

1. Alex/eat/fruit

Alex eats a lot of fruit.
_____

2. James not/drink/milk

_____

3. You not/take/vitamin A

_____

4. Bill eat/chili peppers

_____

5. Rafael not/eat/fish

_____

6. Rick and Sara not/take/vitamins

_____

Cause and Effect with *If (not). . . will*

When you talk about food and health, you often talk about cause and effect. One way to talk about cause and effect is with the expression *if (not) . . . will*.

Example: **If** you do**n't** get enough protein, you **will** get sick.
               cause   **effect**

If you are not sure about an effect, use the word *can* instead of *will*. (*Can* means "it is possible.")

Example: **If** you do**n't** take enough vitamins, you **can** get sick.

E. CAUSE AND EFFECT WITH *IF (NOT) . . . WILL* Combine each cause and effect with *if (not) . . . will/can*. Write your sentences on the lines.

1.   too many cookies   get sick

   If you eat too many cookies, you will get sick.

2.   not enough vitamins   feel tired

   _____

3.   a lot of vegetables   feel good

   _____

4.   too much coffee   become nervous

   _____

5.   a lot of milk   have strong bones

   _____

F. REVIEW/EDITING Read the following paragraph. There are at least six mistakes in it. These are mistakes with the count and noncount nouns, quantity expressions, and cause/effect statements. Find and correct them.

Can you eat a̶ nutritious food at a fast-food restaurant? The experts disagree, but some say that if you eat too many fast food, you not have a well-balanced diet. Other nutritionists say that if you make a good choices, you can eat well at a fast-food restaurant. These experts have the following recommendations: Don't add extra sauces, too many cheese, or bacons to your burger. Try your burger with lettuces, onion, and tomato, instead. And most importantly, order small or medium sizes—not "super sizes."

PART ⑤ ACADEMIC WRITING

WRITING ASSIGNMENT

In Part 5, you will write a paragraph of analysis about a diet. Is it a healthy diet?

STEP A. Choose one of the following diets to write about:
- your own diet
- a friend's diet
- a cultural diet (for example, Asian, Latin, Mediterranean)
- a vegetarian diet
- a diet to lose weight

STEP B. PLANNING YOUR PARAGRAPH Answer the following questions on a separate piece of paper. Write only short notes, not complete sentences.

1. What foods are in this diet? List them. Include drinks.

2. What nutrients are in these foods and drinks? Do they contain a lot of protein? Fat? Carbohydrates? Vitamins? Which ones? Minerals? Which ones?
   Note: In this context, *protein* and *fat* are noncount nouns. For example: Chicken has a lot of *protein*.

3. What is your opinion of this diet? Is it good or bad?

4. What are the reasons for your opinion? Give at least two reasons.

5. Explain how each reason supports your opinion. Use *If (not) . . . will* statements.

Writing Strategy

Organizing a Paragraph of Analysis

There are many ways to organize an analysis paragraph. The following order shows one way.

Step 1: State your opinion about the subject. This is your topic sentence.

Step 2: Give a reason to support your opinion.

Step 3: Explain how the reason supports your opinion. This is the analysis.

You can repeat Steps 2 and 3 in the same paragraph if you have more than one reason.

Example:

Tony doesn't have a very healthy diet. His diet isn't healthy because he eats a lot of butter and cheese every day. Butter and cheese contain a lot of fat. If you eat too much fat, your body will not use it, and you will gain weight. Extra weight is bad for your health. Also, Tony doesn't eat enough fruits and vegetables. Fruits and vegetables contain vitamins. If you don't get enough vitamins, you can get sick. For example, if you don't get enough vitamin C, you can get skin diseases.

STEP C. WRITING THE PARAGRAPH Use your notes from Step B. Write complete sentences in paragraph form. You might make some mistakes, but don't worry about them at this point.

Test-Taking Strategy

Checking Your Work

When you write a paragraph or an essay for a test, leave some time to check for mistakes before you turn it in. Re-read it. Did you use correct punctuation? Are all your sentences on the topic? Do you have good examples? Make your corrections quickly.

STEP D. EDITING Read your paragraph and look for mistakes. Look for:
- paragraph form (indentation, margins)
- the topic sentence
- the use of reasons to support your opinion
- count and noncount nouns
- quantity expressions
- cause/effect statements

STEP E. REWRITING Write your paragraph again, without the mistakes.

UNIT **2** VOCABULARY WORKSHOP

Review vocabulary that you learned in Chapters 3 and 4.

A. MATCHING Match the definitions to the words. Write the correct letters on the lines.

_____ **1.** apes   **a.** insects

_____ **2.** aquatic   **b.** gorillas and chimpanzees

_____ **3.** aristocrats   **c.** wealthy people

_____ **4.** behavior   **d.** movements with the hands

_____ **5.** blink   **e.** living in water

_____ **6.** bugs   **f.** animals that feed their babies milk

_____ **7.** distinct   **g.** the way that an animal acts

_____ **8.** gestures   **h.** specific and different from others

_____ **9.** instinct   **i.** close and open the eyes quickly

_____ **10.** mammals   **j.** something that we know without being taught

B. TRUE OR FALSE? Which sentences are true? Which are false? Fill in Ⓣ for *True* or Ⓕ for *False*.

1. A dog might **salivate** when he smells food.   Ⓣ   Ⓕ

2. **Pesticides** are carbohydrates that the body needs.   Ⓣ   Ⓕ

3. A **dolphin** looks like a fish but is really a mammal.   Ⓣ   Ⓕ

4. Animals kept in a zoo are not in their natural **habitat**.   Ⓣ   Ⓕ

5. Many animals that live **in captivity** live in zoos.   Ⓣ   Ⓕ

6. Most dogs like to **fetch** balls.   Ⓣ   Ⓕ

7. You can find meat in the **dairy** section of a supermarket.   Ⓣ   Ⓕ

8. Scientists who specialize in mammals study **entomology**.   Ⓣ   Ⓕ

C. WORDS IN PHRASES Write the words from the box on the lines below to complete the phrases.

acids	error	movements	products	response

1. body _____

2. fight-or-flight _____

3. trial and _____

4. fatty _____

5. dairy _____

D. FREQUENTLY USED WORDS Some of the most common words in English are in the box below. They are among the most frequently used 500–1,000 words. Fill in the blanks with words from the box. (You'll use some words twice.) When you finish, check your answers in the second paragraph on page 71.

arms	floor	human	off	pull	strong	watching
exist	glass	natural	opinion	rocks	watched	

With its eight powerful _____ arms _____, an octopus can swim backwards or

_____ itself over _____ on the ocean
2   3

_____. An octopus is very _____, but is it intelligent?
4   5

People at the Hellabrunn Zoo, in Germany, might have an _____ about this.
6

_____ jars do not _____ in the ocean, the
7   8

_____ environment of an octopus, so you might not expect an octopus to
9

know how to open one. However, at the Hellabrunn Zoo, an octopus named Frieda had the

motivation to learn how to open a jar. The motivation was food. Frieda _____
10

her _____ keepers as they opened _____ jars with
11   12

food inside. From _____ them, she learned how to twist
13

_____ the lid and reach inside for the food.
14

UNIT**3**

○○○○○○ U.S. HISTORY

Chapter 5
From Settlement to Independence: 1607–1776

Chapter 6
A Changing Nation: 1850–1900

From Settlement to Independence: 1607–1776

Discuss these questions:
- Look at the picture. When did people wear clothes like this?
- When did Europeans start coming to America?
- Who lived in America before the Europeans?
- Read the chapter title. What do you think the chapter will be about?

BEFORE READING

👥 **THINKING AHEAD** Look at the pictures. Discuss these questions with a partner.

1. What are the people doing?

2. Who are the people in the pictures? How did they live?

3. What was America like before the Europeans arrived?

READING

Read about some of the people who lived in Colonial America—that is, America at the time when Great Britain* controlled the land. By 1750, Great Britain had thirteen **colonies** (areas that are controlled by a country that is far away) in America. As you read, think about these questions:

• Where did most Colonial Americans come from?
• Why did most Colonial Americans move to America?

*Also called England or Britain.

People in Colonial America

The English

About 60 percent of the Europeans in Colonial America were English (British). The first English arrived in Jamestown (now in Virginia) in 1607, and by the 1730s there were thirteen colonies along the Atlantic coast. Most people were Protestant—a religious group. The colonists came for religious freedom—the freedom to practice
5   religion in their own way. Most of them came from middle-class families. Many colonists were farmers, blacksmiths, stonecutters, or carpenters. A few were wealthy and worked as doctors, lawyers, and religious leaders.

Other Europeans

The rest of the settlers (people who came to live permanently) in America came mainly from Scotland, Germany, Holland, France, Sweden, and Finland. Most came
10   in the early 1700s. They came to the colonies for a better, safer, and more peaceful life. Many came to escape war, hunger, or bad treatment. Some people, for example the French Protestants, came for religious freedom. Like the English, many were farmers; others worked as weavers, potters, and artists.

Some Common English Names

Many common English names come from the jobs that people did.		
Name:	Smith	Potter	Weaver
Job:	A blacksmith	A potter	A weaver

Many common English names come from the jobs that people did.		
Name:	Cooper	Stone

Job:	A cooper*	A stonecutter

*A cooper is a person who makes barrels.

Africans

There were 20 Africans in the colonies in 1619. By the end of the 1600s, slave traders kidnapped—captured and took by force—thousands more and brought them to the colonies. The Africans came to America on crowded slave ships. There was little food. Many people died. For those who survived, all their freedom was taken away from them, and they were forced to work without pay, usually on large farms called plantations.

Source: *America Is* (Drewry and O'Connor)

Slave traders with African slaves

AFTER READING

A. CHECK YOUR UNDERSTANDING What three groups of people lived in Colonial America? Where did they come from? Why did they come to the colonies? What did they do in the colonies? Complete the chart below.

Who were they? Where did they come from?	Why did they come to the colonies?	What did they do in the colonies?
The English; England		
	They wanted a better, safer, and more peaceful life.	
		They were slaves.

 B. MAKING INFERENCES Discuss these questions with a partner:
- What was life probably like in Europe in the early 1700s?
- What was life like for most Africans in the colonies?

C. APPLYING INFORMATION In small groups, discuss these questions:
- Weaver, Cooper, and Smith are common English names that come from jobs. Do any family names in your native language come from jobs that people did a long time ago? If yes, what are they?

Famous Colonial Americans

BEFORE READING

Picture A: A colonial home

Picture B: Slave quarters

A. THINKING AHEAD Look at the pictures. They show two typical Colonial American homes. In small groups, discuss the questions:

1. How did the people in each picture probably live?

   Example: The people in Picture A probably lived a good life with nice food and warm clothes.

2. How much freedom did the people in each picture have?

3. What rights do you think they had?

B. PREVIEWING Look at the title of the reading below. Do you know the names of the two people? If yes, tell a partner what you know about each person. If no, think of three questions about each person.

Now look at the pictures and the captions in the reading and answer these questions.

1. What is one thing that Benjamin Franklin probably did in his life?

2. What is one thing that Phillis Wheatley probably did in her life?

Reading Strategy

Guessing the Meanings of New Words: Using an Explanation in the Next Sentence

You don't always need a dictionary to learn the meanings of new words. Sometimes there is an explanation or a definition of a new word in the sentence following the word.

Example: Benjamin Franklin was **curious** about everything. He was especially interested in electricity.

C. GUESSING THE MEANINGS OF NEW WORDS As you read, look for explanations of new words in the next sentences.

READING

Read about two famous Colonial Americans. As you read, highlight the answers to these questions:
• How were Benjamin Franklin and Phillis Wheatley different from each other?
• How were they similar to each other?

Famous Colonial Americans: Benjamin Franklin and Phillis Wheatley

Benjamin Franklin and Phillis Wheatley were two famous Colonial Americans. They were different from each other in many ways: one was a middle-class white man born in Boston, Massachusetts; the other was a female slave born in Senegal, Africa. However, both were successful,
5 creative individuals, and both had strong feelings about American independence.

Benjamin Franklin

Benjamin Franklin was born into a large family in Boston, Massachusetts, in 1706. When he was a child, his parents made him work in their soap and candle shop. But Franklin didn't
10 like that kind of work. He was very smart and had big ideas, so he went to work as a printer in his brother's printing shop.

Benjamin Franklin

In colonial times, printers published all kinds of things: newspapers, books, pamphlets (very short books without covers), and even playing cards. Franklin enjoyed the printing business, but he also loved to write. Soon he was printing his own essays.

15　　Later, Franklin moved to Philadelphia and started his own printing business. In Philadelphia, he published a newspaper, *The Pennsylvania Gazette*, and dozens of his own essays, pamphlets, and articles. He even published his autobiography. Surprisingly, he wrote this story of his own life although he was still a young man. Franklin also published a book that he wrote called *Poor Richard's Almanack* and the very first novel 20　ever printed in America—*Pamela*, by Samuel Richardson.

　　Franklin retired from the printing business when he was in his forties. After he stopped working, he spent time on his other interests: science, inventions, and politics. Franklin was curious about everything. He was especially interested in electricity. He had a theory. His idea was that lightning was really 25　electricity. To prove this, he performed his famous kite experiment: he attached a piece of metal to the top of a kite, a key to the kite string, and flew the kite during a storm. When lightning hit the piece of metal on the kite, 30　Franklin touched the key. When he got a shock, he knew that his theory was correct.

Franklin's kite experiment

　　In his lifetime, Franklin invented many useful things. One of his inventions was the lightning rod, a metal pole on the top of a 35　building. During a thunderstorm it attracts lightning and keeps the building and the people inside it safe.

　　In 1751, Franklin joined the Pennsylvania Assembly. This began his career in politics. 40　Soon he became interested in uniting the colonies. Like many people, he thought the colonies should join together under one government and separate from England. In 1776, he helped write the *Declaration of Independence*.

　　After the War for Independence (1775-1783), Franklin helped form the new American government. He worked to end slavery (although he wasn't successful), and 45　continued to invent things. He died in 1790 at the age of 84.

Phillis Wheatley

　　Not many women were well-known during colonial times, and almost no women became published poets. However, there were some exceptions. Unlike most slave women, Phillis Wheatley received an education. She also became a popular poet in both England and America.

50　　Phillis Wheatley was born in Senegal, Africa in about 1753. In 1761, John and Susannah Wheatley bought her as a slave in Boston. The Wheatleys taught her to read and write. This was unusual: most slave owners did not want to educate their slaves. Phillis also learned history, geography, and Latin.

Phillis wrote her first poem at the age of thirteen. It was about the king of England, George III (the Third), and how happy people were when he canceled a very unpopular law in the colonies called the Stamp Act. The poem was so good that the Wheatleys gave Phillis less work to do and let her spend most of her time writing.

The Wheatleys gave Phillis her freedom in 1773, and she went to England where she met other writers. Her first book, *Poems on Various Subjects Religious and Moral*, was published. At that time, there weren't many books of poetry by Americans, and this was the first one by a black woman.

Many of Phillis' poems were about her religious beliefs and about slavery. Phillis was also interested in independence for the colonies, and she admired George Washington. In April 1776, she wrote a poem to Washington. It was published in the *Pennsylvania Magazine*. Washington read the poem and asked to meet Phillis.

After Phillis returned from England, people stopped reading her poetry. Unfortunately, she died poor and unknown.

Source: *America Is* (Drewry and O'Connor)

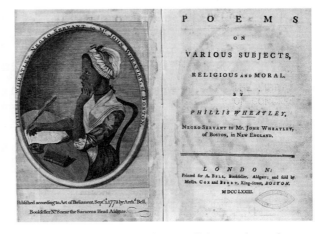

Poems on Various Subjects Religious and Moral
by Phillis Wheatley

AFTER READING

A. CHECK YOUR UNDERSTANDING Fill in the chart with information about Benjamin Franklin and Phillis Wheatley.

	Benjamin Franklin	**Phillis Wheatley**
Born where?	Boston	
Born when?		
Lived where?		
Died when?		1784
Interests		
Accomplishments		

Critical Thinking Strategy

Using a Venn Diagram to Show Similarities and Differences

A Venn diagram is a type of graphic organizer. It is a good way to show similarities and differences. Look at the Venn diagram below. It is a comparison of two groups of people who lived in the English colonies.

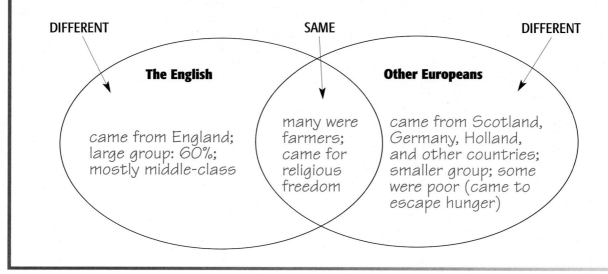

DIFFERENT   SAME   DIFFERENT

The English

came from England; large group: 60%; mostly middle-class

many were farmers; came for religious freedom

Other Europeans

came from Scotland, Germany, Holland, and other countries; smaller group; some were poor (came to escape hunger)

B. USING A VENN DIAGRAM TO SHOW SIMILARITIES AND DIFFERENCES With a partner, use the Venn diagram to answer the prereading questions:

• How were Benjamin Franklin and Phillis Wheatley different from each other?
• How were they similar to each other?

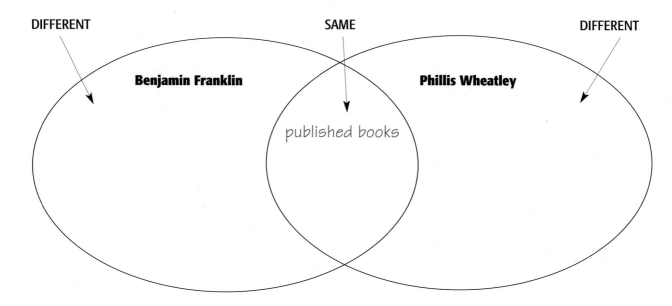

DIFFERENT   SAME   DIFFERENT

Benjamin Franklin

Phillis Wheatley

published books

C. VOCABULARY CHECK Look back at the reading on pages 125–127. Look for words and phrases that have explanations in the next sentence. Highlight the words and definitions in the reading. Then write the correct words and phrases on the lines.

1. a place where people print and publish
   material such as books and newspapers (Lines 11–14)   *printing shop*

2. a story of the author's own life (Lines 17–18)   _____

3. stopped working (Lines 21–22)   _____

4. an idea about something (Line 24)   _____

5. a metal pole that keeps a building safe in a storm (Lines 34–37)   _____

6. joining together (Lines 40–41)   _____

7. unlike most (people) (Lines 47–48)   _____

D. REVIEW: UNDERSTANDING PRONOUNS What do the pronouns in red refer to? Write the correct references on the lines.

1. Phillis Wheatley wrote her first poem at the age of thirteen. **It** was about the king of England.

   It = _____*poem*_____

2. Benjamin Franklin and Phillis Wheatley were two famous Colonial Americans. **They** were different from each other in many ways.

   They = _____

3. Franklin enjoyed the printing business, but **he** also loved to write.

   he = _____

4. In April 1776, she wrote a poem about Washington. **It** was published in the *Pennsylvania Magazine*.

   it = _____

E. APPLYING YOUR KNOWLEDGE In small groups, discuss these questions.

1. Can you think of another person similar to Benjamin Franklin in the history of another country?

2. Can you think of another person similar to Phillis Wheatley in the history of another country?

PART 3 ACADEMIC READING The Road to Rebellion

BEFORE READING

A. VOCABULARY PREPARATION Read the sentences below. The words in red are from the next reading. Circle the correct part of speech for each word in red. Circle *n* for a noun or *v* for a verb. Then try to guess the meanings of the words from the context. Write your guesses on the lines. Do not use a dictionary.

                                                                    Parts of Speech

1. The Navigation Acts allowed the colonists to **trade** only   n   v
   with Great Britain. They could not buy or sell goods with
   any other countries.

   Guess: _____

2. England sent soldiers to the colonies and made sure that   n   v
   people did not try to **smuggle** goods—take things into the
   country secretly.

   Guess: _____

3. Colonists couldn't directly change the laws, but they could   n   v
   protest—speak or act against things that they disagreed with.

   Guess: _____

4. After some time, the British **repealed** (canceled) the   n   v
   Stamp Act in 1766.

   Guess: _____

5. The Americans wrote a letter to King George III that listed   n   v
   their **grievances**—the things that they were angry about.

   Guess: _____

Now compare your answers with a partner's answers. If your answers are different, look up the words in a dictionary.

Reading Strategy

Previewing: Scanning for Years

Scanning—quickly searching a reading to find specific information—is a very important reading strategy. Years (such as *1776* or *2001*) are important in history. Scanning for years *before* you read is a good way to preview a reading. In a reading you can easily find years because they look different from words.

B. SCANNING FOR YEARS Scan the reading on pages 132–133 and write all the years that you can find on the lines below.

_____   _____

_____   _____

_____   _____

_____

Reading Strategy

Previewing: Scanning for Events

In history, what happened on a certain date—an event—is also important. Some of the important events in the next reading are acts (or laws) that the British government passed. Most of these acts have special names. They're easy to find because they're capitalized (for example, the *Navigation Acts*). Scanning for events *before* you read is another good way to preview a reading.

C. SCANNING FOR EVENTS Scan the reading. Look for the acts that the British government passed. Write the acts on the lines below.

_____   _____

_____   _____

_____   _____

_____   _____

D. THINKING AHEAD Before you read the passage, discuss these questions with a partner.

1. What are some advantages of living in a colony?

2. What are some disadvantages of living in a colony?

3. What are some reasons that colonists might not want to have another country control them?

READING

Read about the American Revolution. As you read, think about this question:
• Why did the American colonists want to be independent from Great Britain?

The Road to Rebellion

For many years, the British government was too busy to control the American colonies carefully. There were political problems within Great Britain and many wars with France. But after 1763, Great Britain was at peace. It
5 decided to do two things: become stricter—have more rules—with the American colonies and raise money in the colonies to pay its war debts. In order to do these things, Great Britain passed some
10 new laws.

A British soldier

In 1763, the British government passed laws for the colonies called the Grenville Acts. One of these laws forced the colonists to obey the Navigation Acts.
15 These laws (passed in the 1600s) allowed the colonists to trade only with Great Britain. The colonists could not buy or sell goods with any other countries. Another new law was the Sugar Act. This law
20 forced the colonists to pay a tax on sugar, wine, and coffee. Another law was the Stamp Act. It required colonists to pay a tax on all printed material, such as newspapers, stamps, and even playing cards.

At the same time, Great Britain sent soldiers to the colonies. The soldiers policed the colonies and made sure people did not try to smuggle goods—bring
25 things into the country secretly—to avoid paying the new taxes. To take care of these soldiers, Great Britain passed the Quartering Act. This law required the colonists to give the soldiers food, supplies, and places to stay.

These laws made the colonists very angry. For one thing, all the tax money went directly to the British government. Americans did not have representation in—could
30 not vote for members of—the Parliament in England. Therefore, the colonists could not say how the government should spend their tax money. They also could not change laws. The colonists called this "taxation without representation."

They couldn't directly change the laws, but they could protest—speak or act against things that they disagreed with. For example, the colonists boycotted
35 British goods. They refused to buy these goods to protest the Stamp Act. After some time, the boycott worked; the British repealed (canceled) the Stamp Act in 1766.

But the British government still needed money. So in 1767, a new Parliament leader, Charles Townshend, passed more laws. These were the Townshend Acts. They required the colonists to pay more taxes—on lead, paint, paper, glass, and tea. At the same time, the government passed a law that allowed writs of assistance—documents that allowed officials to search the colonists' property whenever they wanted.

A Patriot

The colonists protested again. They boycotted British goods once more, and they wrote letters to Parliament. The colonists began to form two groups: the Patriots and the Loyalists. The Patriots wanted independence from England; the Loyalists wanted America to remain a British colony. One Patriot group was in Boston, Massachusetts. They were called the Sons of Liberty. This group organized boycotts and protests.

After some years, Great Britain repealed—canceled—all of the Townshend taxes except the one on tea. In 1773, the British government passed a new Tea Act. This law forced the colonies to buy their tea from one company only, the British East India Company. In addition, this law allowed the company to charge very high prices for its tea. People throughout the colonies protested. They boycotted tea. The Sons of Liberty went further: they went on board three British tea ships in Boston Harbor late at night. They dumped more than 300 crates of British tea into the water. This was called the Boston Tea Party.

The British leaders were shocked by the Boston Tea Party. They passed new laws in 1774 called the Intolerable Acts. These acts punished the colony of Massachusetts by closing Boston Harbor. In other words, no ships could enter or leave the colony from Boston Harbor. The people suffered.

The Intolerable Acts made most colonists want to break with Great Britain. They formed the Continental Congress. This was a group of representatives from every colony except Georgia. At first, the representatives had one purpose: to discuss ways to deal with the British government. They wrote a letter to King George III. In it they listed their grievances—things that they were angry about. They also organized another boycott of British goods. However, King George and most British leaders would not give in. By early 1776, the idea of independence was gaining strong support throughout the colonies.

Source: *America Is* (Drewry and O'Connor)

AFTER READING

 A. MAIN IDEA In small groups, discuss this question:
• What was the main reason that the American colonists wanted to be independent from Great Britain?

Reading Strategy

Making a Timeline

Timelines are a type of graphic organizer. Timelines are one way to show chronological (time) order. When you read about history, making a timeline can help you identify and remember important events.

 B. MAKING A TIMELINE Go back to the reading on pages 132–133 and the list of years and events you found before you read (page 131). Match the acts with the years. Write the acts on the correct lines in the timeline.

Timeline

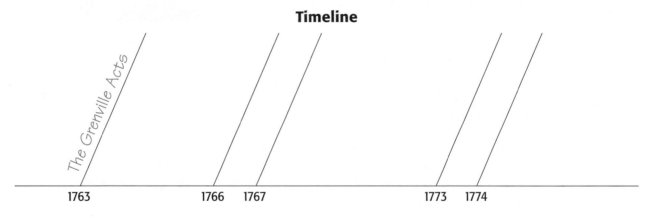

1763   1766   1767   1773   1774

C. UNDERSTANDING DETAILS Without going back to the reading, match the acts with their descriptions. Write the correct letters on the lines.

_____ **1.** Quartering Act   **a.** a tax on printed material

_____ **2.** Stamp Act   **b.** a tax on tea

_____ **3.** Townshend Acts   **c.** taxes on lead, paint, paper, glass, and tea

_____ **4.** Tea Act   **d.** closed Boston Harbor

_____ **5.** Intolerable Acts   **e.** colonists had to give British soldiers food, supplies, and a place to stay

Now go back to the reading on pages 132–133 to check your answers.

D. VOCABULARY CHECK Look back at the reading on pages 132–133 to find words and phrases for the following definitions. Write the correct words and phrases on the lines.

1. refused to buy something (Lines 34–35): _____

2. documents that allowed British officials to search colonists' property whenever they wanted (Lines 41–44): _____

3. a group of colonists who wanted independence from England (Lines 49–50): _____

4. a group of colonists who wanted America to remain a colony (Lines 50–52): _____

E. CAUSE AND EFFECT The British passed several laws. This made the colonists angry, and they reacted. Then the British passed more laws. Complete the cause-effect graphic organizer to show British actions and colonist reactions. Use the events in the box.

Actions	**Reactions**
act repealed	the Boston Tea Party
the Intolerable Acts	boycott
~~the Stamp Act~~	~~idea of independence~~
~~the Tea Act~~	

British Actions   **Colonists' Reactions**

_____ the Stamp Act _____   ————————➤   _____

_____   ◄————————

_____ the Tea Act _____   ————————➤   _____

_____   ◄———————— ————————➤   _idea of independence_

F. MAKING CONNECTIONS Use the information from this chapter to answer this question with a partner.

- In your opinion, how might the British laws passed between 1763 and 1774 have affected the following people?

a slave	Phillis Wheatley	a merchant
a farmer	Benjamin Franklin	a plantation owner

G. APPLICATION In small groups, discuss another country's history. Was this country ever a colony? If yes, how did it become independent? Did this country ever colonize another area? If yes, how did that area become independent?

H. WORD JOURNAL Go back to the readings in Parts 1, 2, and 3. Which words are important for *you* to remember? Put them in your Word Journal.

I. JOURNAL WRITING Choose one of these topics:

- Imagine you are a captured African. It is 1700. You have just landed in America. How do you feel? What do you think your life will be like now?
- Imagine you are a middle-class English person. It is 1700. You have just landed in America. How do you feel? What do you think your life will be like now?
- Imagine you are a Native American. It is 1700. Europeans have just landed near your home. How do you feel? What do you think your life will be like now?

Write for 10 minutes. Don't worry about grammar. Don't use a dictionary.

PART ④ THE MECHANICS OF WRITING

In Part 4, you will practice using the simple past, causatives, and also paraphrasing and condensing information. You will need this knowledge in Part 5 to write a paragraph summarizing one of the chapter readings.

A. REVIEW: SIMPLE PAST Write five sentences about an event or a famous person in history. Use five verbs from the box below. Use at least two negatives (*did + not + verb*).

arrive	become	buy	live	receive	sell	unite	work

1. _____

2. _____

3. _____

4. _____

5. _____

Can and *Could*

You use *can* + the simple form of a verb to say someone is able to do something now.

Example: Today, all Americans **can vote** when they are 18 years old.

To talk about ability in the past, you use *could* + the simple form of the verb.

Example: In Colonial America, only white males **could vote**.

Negative	**Contraction**
Children **cannot** vote.	Children **can't** vote.
Colonial women **could not** vote.	Colonial women **couldn't** vote.

B. *CAN* AND *COULD* What can (or can't) people do now? What could (or couldn't) people do in the past? Write four sentences—two about the present and two about the past.

1. _____

2. _____

3. _____

4. _____

Causatives: *Force* and *Make*

Use **causatives** to talk about someone causing someone else to do something. When you talk or write about Colonial America, you may need to use causatives. Two causatives are *force* and *make*.

Force is used with a noun, *to*, and a verb (*force* + noun + *to* + verb).

Example: England **forced the colonists to pay** a tax on sugar.

Make is used with a noun and a verb (*make* + noun + verb). Do not use *to* with *make*.

Example: England also **made the colonists pay** a tax on stamps.

Note: The past form of *force* is *forced*. The past form of *make* is *made*.

C. CAUSATIVES Use the following cues to make sentences. Use *force* or *make* and the simple past.

1. (force) England/the colonists/buy English tea

England forced the colonists to buy English tea.

2. (make) Great Britain/the colonists/pay a tax on newspapers

_____

3. (force) The Sugar Act/the colonists/pay a tax on sugar

_____

4. (make) English laws/the colonists/want independence

_____

5. (force) A Virginia law/African servants/become slaves

_____

Test-Taking Strategy

Paraphrasing

On a standardized test, you may be asked to read a passage and then write about what you have just read. Being able to quickly paraphrase is an important test-taking strategy.

Paraphrasing is restating information in different words. When you paraphrase, you do not change the information. There are many ways to give information in different words. One way is to replace words and expressions with synonyms—words with the same meaning. Do not change words that don't have synonyms.

Example: Original: On Thanksgiving, people celebrated with festive meals and public games.

Paraphrase: On Thanksgiving, people had special meals and events.

Notice that the paraphrase has the same meaning. However, it contains synonymous words and expressions.

- *people celebrated* ⟶ **people had**
- *festive meals* ⟶ **special meals**
- *public games* ⟶ **events**

D. PARAPHRASING Paraphrase the sentences below. Use synonyms and synonymous expressions whenever possible.

1. Many Europeans came to America for religious freedom.

Many Europeans settled in America because they wanted the freedom to practice religion their own way.

2. Some Europeans came to escape war, hunger, or bad treatment.

_____

_____

3. Slave traders kidnapped many Africans and brought them to the colonies.

_____

_____

4. Religion was important to Colonial Americans.

_____

_____

5. Africans belonged to Europeans and worked for no pay.

_____

_____

Summary Writing: Condensing

When you write a summary, you keep the main ideas of the original material. However, you explain the ideas in many fewer sentences. In order to do this, you must condense. **Condensing** means making smaller or shorter.

Example: Original: The family was an important part of Colonial America. Most colonial families were very large. An average family had fourteen or more members. Farming families had many children because there was a lot of work to do. Also, people often died at an early age because of war, sickness, and little or no medical care.

Condensed Version: Most colonial farming families were very large because there was a lot of work to do and because people often died young.

Notice the following:

• The condensed version says the same thing as the original.

• Specific details are left out. For example, the information in this sentence: *An average family had fourteen or more members* does not appear in the condensed version.

• The original version contains five sentences. The condensed version is only one sentence.

• The condensed version uses synonymous words and expressions.

   Example: *people often died at an early age* ⟶ **people often died young**

• The condensed version uses conjunctions (words that join sentences, such as *because* and *and*) to connect ideas.

E. CONDENSING For each group of sentences, write one new sentence. The new sentence must include the same information as the original. Use synonymous words and expressions.

1. **Original**: Most of the white settlers in the English colonies worked as farmers. Others were merchants.

   Condensed version: In the colonies, most white settlers were farmers or merchants.

   _____

2. **Original**: Many people who came to the English colonies did not arrive as farmers, merchants, artisans, or manufacturers. They came as indentured servants.

   Condensed version: _____

   _____

3. **Original**: There was time in the evenings for fun. People told stories or read aloud. They also played games or sang songs.

   Condensed version: _____

   _____

4. Original: Many people who came to the English colonies did not arrive as farmers, merchants, artisans, or manufacturers. They came as indentured servants. Indentured servants did not pay their way to America. Someone else paid it. When they arrived, they had to work for this person.

Condensed version: _____

_____

5. Original: The colonists lived under English law. According to English law, women had few political rights. For example, they could not vote. They usually could not own property. However, most women worked hard, especially those who lived on farms.

Condensed version: _____

_____

F. REVIEW/EDITING Read the paragraph. There are at least six mistakes in it. These are mistakes with the simple past, *can* and *could*, and *force* and *make*. Find and correct the mistakes.

                             were
Most Africans in North America ~~was~~ slaves. They live on plantations. They have very hard lives.

Some Africans did housework, but most work in the fields. The large plantation owners hired

overseers, or bosses. The overseers made the slaves to work hard. There were many rules for slaves.

Slaves cannot leave the plantation without permission from their master (owner). They cannot learn to

read or write.

Source: Adapted from *The American Journey*

PART 5 ACADEMIC WRITING

WRITING ASSIGNMENT

In Part 5, you will write a one-paragraph summary of a reading in this chapter.

STEP A. CHOOSING A TOPIC Choose one of the readings in this chapter to summarize:
• "People in Colonial America" (pages 121–122)
• "Phillis Wheatley," the second section of "Famous Colonial Americans" (pages 125–127)
• "The Road to Rebellion" (pages 132–133)

Writing Strategy

Writing a Summary

Here is one way to write a summary. For each paragraph (or the most important paragraphs) of the original, write one sentence with the main idea of that paragraph. You must paraphrase and condense in order to do this.

Here are some characteristics of a good summary:

• The summary is shorter than the original version.

• The summary says the same thing as the original version. In other words, it paraphrases the original version.

• The topic sentence gives the main idea of the summary.

• The summary leaves out unimportant details.

• The ideas are not necessarily in the same order as in the original version. (If necessary, you can change the order of the ideas in the original version to organize them more logically.)

Example: This is a summary of the first part of "Famous Colonial Americans." (The numbers in parentheses after each sentence show the lines that the information comes from. **Note:** Don't include these numbers in your summary.)

Benjamin Franklin was a successful, creative American who cared about American independence. (4–6) Franklin didn't like the profession his family chose for him, so he went to work in his brother's printing shop. (8–11) He discovered that he loved to write and later started his own printing business. There he published many things, including his own writings. (14–15) When he retired from the printing business, he spent time doing experiments with electricity and inventing useful things, such as the lightning rod. (22–38) In 1751, he became involved in politics. He worked for American independence and helped to form the new American government. (38–45)

STEP B. PLANNING YOUR PARAGRAPH Answer the questions on a separate piece of paper. Write only short notes, not complete sentences.

1. Re-read the passage that you chose. What is the main idea of the entire passage? (This will be the topic sentence of your summary.)

2. What is the main idea of the first paragraph? Write it in one sentence. Use paraphrasing and condensing.

3. What is the main idea of the next paragraph? Write it in one sentence. Use paraphrasing and condensing.

Repeat Question 3 for each important paragraph in the original passage.

STEP C. WRITING THE PARAGRAPH Use your notes from Step B. Write complete sentences in paragraph form. You might make some mistakes, but don't worry about them at this point.

STEP D. EDITING Read your paragraph and look for mistakes. Look for:
• paragraph form (indentation, margins)
• the topic sentence
• tenses
• *can* and *could*
• causatives (*make* and *force*)
• paraphrasing
• condensing

STEP E. REWRITING Write your paragraph again, without the mistakes.

CHAPTER 6

A Changing Nation: 1850–1900

Discuss these questions:

- Look at the picture. The women are in a movie about immigrants in America. What countries do you think they came from?
- What other countries do American immigrants come from?
- How can immigration change a country?
- Read the chapter title. What do you think the chapter will be about?

BEFORE READING

Native-American* village

"Wild West" town

Immigrant neighborhood

*In the past, it was common to call Native Americans *Indians* or *American Indians*. Today most people use the term *Native Americans*.

THINKING AHEAD Look at the pictures. Discuss these questions with a partner.

1. Describe each picture. What do you see?

2. Who are the people in the photos? What kind of work did they do? What kind of lives did they have?

READING

Read the quotations about American life in the second half of the 19th century. You won't understand every word, but try to get a feeling for the times that they describe. As you read, think about this question:
• What can you learn about U.S. history (1850–1900) from these people?

Voices from the Past

A log house

 . . . a log house . . . one hundred miles from a railroad, forty miles from the nearest post office, and half a dozen miles from any neighbors save [except for] Indians, wolves,
5 and wildcats.

— Nicolas Stott Shaw, 1859

When you first came we were very many, and you were few; now you are many, and we are getting very few, and we are poor.
10 — Red Cloud, Chief of the Teton Sioux, 1870

The firing of guns in and around town was so continuous that it reminded me of a Fourth of July celebration. There was shooting when I got up and when I went to bed.

— resident of Newton, Kansas, 1871

15

Chief Joseph

I am tired of fighting. Our chiefs are killed . . . The old men are all dead. It is the young men who now say yes or no. He who led the young men is dead. It is cold and we have no blankets. The little children are freezing to
20 death. My people—some of them have run away to the hills and have no blankets and no food. No one knows where they are . . . I want to have time to look for my children and see how many of them I can find. Maybe I shall find
25 them among the dead. Hear me, my chiefs, my heart is sick and sad . . . From where the sun now stands Joseph will fight no more.

— Chief Joseph, 1877

30 The western country is rapidly filling up . . . Immigration is following the railroad lines and then spreading right and left . . . What is to become of the Indians?

— Carl Schurz, Secretary of the Interior, 1881

35 Here it is not asked what or who was your father, but the question is, what are you?

— Scandinavian immigrant in Minnesota, 19th century

I was thrilled with the realization of what this freedom of education meant. A little girl from across the alley came and offered to conduct us to school . . . We knew the word *school*. We understood . . . the doors stood open for *every* one 40 of us. This incident impressed me more than anything . . .

— Mary Antin, Russian immigrant, 1894

To be a poor man is hard, but to be a poor race in a land of dollars is the very bottom of hardship.

— W.E.B. Du Bois, African-American leader, 1903

AFTER READING

A. MAKING INFERENCES Quotations can help to "paint a picture" of a time and place. In the chart are some inferences about life in the United States from 1850 to 1900. Match the inferences to the quotations in the reading. Write the name of the person who said each quotation in the correct boxes. (Some boxes can have more than one name.)

Inferences	People Who Suggested These Ideas
1. The late 19th century was a terrible time for Native Americans.	Red Cloud, Chief Joseph, Carl Schurz
2. Some towns were exciting but dangerous.	
3. For some people, life was very lonely.	
4. The railroad (trains) brought big changes to the western states.	
5. Immigration to the United States gave some people hope.	
6. The Native-American population went down during this time.	
7. Americans thought, "The present is more important than the past."	

Interpreting Graphs

Many textbooks contain graphs with information that supports the text. Usually, a graph is more specific than the text that it supports. That is, a graph gives more details. There are two examples of graphs below. Graphs are useful because they can help you to "see" information.

B. COMPARING GRAPHS ABOUT POPULATION CHANGE Look at these graphs of population in the United States from 1850 to 1900. The first graph is about the general population. The second graph is about the Native-American population. Discuss these questions with a partner.

1. What happened to the total population during this time?

2. What happened to the population of Native Americans?

3. Make a guess: why did this happen? (There may be more than one reason.)

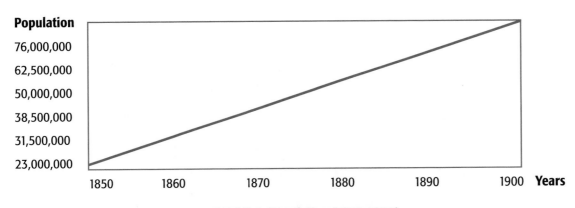

Total U.S. Population (1850–1900)

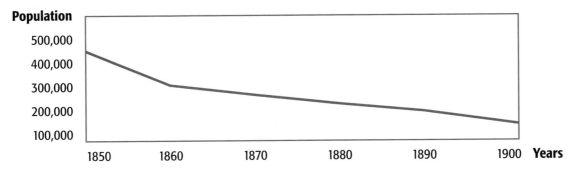

Native-American Population (1850–1900)

C. MAKING CONNECTIONS On page 146 there are historical photographs. On pages 147–148 there are quotations. In small groups, discuss which quotations and photos might belong together.

PART ② GENERAL INTEREST READING
The End of the Frontier

BEFORE READING

Gold miners

Farmers

The buffalo hunt

A. DISCUSSION Look at the pictures. In small groups, discuss these questions.

1. What kind of work did gold miners do?

2. What are some possible problems that farmers had 100 years ago?

3. Why were buffalo important to Native Americans? In what ways did these Native Americans use the buffalo? Think of as many ways as possible.

B. THINKING AHEAD Think about the history of a country that you know well. When did the railroad—trains—connect different parts of the country for the first time? In the chart below, write three ways that the railroad helped this country. Then write three ways that the railroad was bad for this country.

The railroad in _____

(Country)

Good	Bad

Now, in small groups, share your charts.

C. VOCABULARY PREPARATION Read the sentences below. The words in red are from the reading. Try to figure out the new words from the context. Write the meaning of each new word on the line. Do not use a dictionary.

1. From the time of the first colonies, the new Americans were always moving west. They went in search of different things, but the **journey** was long, difficult, and dangerous for everyone.

   A **journey** is a _____.

2. First, miners went west in search of gold or silver. They set up camps. Then other **settlers** came, and a small town grew up around the camp. These settlers started farms or small businesses.

   Settlers are people who _____.

3. Some people moved west to start **ranches**. There were millions of acres of good grassland for the beef cattle to live on, especially in Texas.

   Ranches are places where _____.

4. There were often **droughts**—long periods with no rain.

   Droughts are times when _____.

5. Sometimes billions of insects appeared and ate all the corn, wheat, and other **crops**.

   Examples of **crops** are _____.

D. PREVIEWING Look over the reading on pages 152–153. Write the two headings on the lines. What will the reading be about?

_____   _____

Read about the American West. As you read, don't use a dictionary. Try to guess the meaning of new words. Think about the question below. When you find the answer, highlight it.
• How did the railroad change the western part of the United States?

The End of the Frontier

The Coming of the Railroad

From the time of the first colonies, the new Americans were always moving west, toward the **frontier**—the wild area where there were no European-style towns or cities. Different people were looking for different things:
5 land, freedom, gold, or adventure. The journey to the frontier was long, difficult, and dangerous.

However, something happened to change the journey in the
10 second half of the 19th century. In 1862, two railroad companies raced to build a railroad line across North America. They worked very fast. They received money from
15 the government for each mile of train track (the man-made path a train runs on) that they put down.

Immigrants build the railroad.

Immigrants from Ireland worked for the Union Pacific Company to build from Omaha, Nebraska, toward the west. Immigrants from China worked for the
20 Central Pacific Company to build from Sacramento, California, toward the east. They did all of this work by hand—often in the terrible heat of the desert or in heavy snow high in the mountains. Sometimes they put down 10 miles of track in just one day. On May 10, 1869, the "wedding of the rails" took place in Promontory Point, Utah. It was then possible to travel across North America by
25 train, and the whole country celebrated. Large numbers of people were suddenly able to move west.

Thousand of **miners** moved to Colorado, Nevada, Idaho, Montana, and California. These people went west to dig for gold or silver. In one place after another, the miners set up camp. Other settlers came, and small towns grew
30 around the camps. These settlers started farms or small businesses to supply the miners with food, equipment, and other goods. However, when there was no more gold or silver, people usually moved away, and the empty towns became **ghost towns**.

Other people moved west to start **ranches**. There were millions of acres of
35 good grassland for the beef cattle to live on, especially in Texas. Also, there was

a big market for beef in northern and eastern cities, so for a short time before 1900, cowboys led hundreds of thousands of cattle north on **cattle drives**. These were extremely hard journeys, but they made the cowboy into a hero in stories, songs, and—later—movies.

40   **Homesteaders** moved west, too. These people settled on land because they wanted to farm it. In 1862, Congress passed the Homestead Act. This law gave 160 acres of land to a family after they lived on it for five years. Most of these farms were on the Great Plains—huge spaces of flat land in the Midwest. Life on the plains was very hard. In summer, temperatures were over 100° F

45 (38° C). In winter, there was a lot of snow. Often there were also droughts— long periods with no rain. Sometimes billions of insects appeared and ate all the corn, wheat, and other crops. Also, it was a lonely life; the nearest neighbor was usually many, many miles away.

The End of the Native Americans' Way of Life

50   The way of life of the Native Americans—that is, the Indians—changed forever when the railroad crossed the Great Plains and brought the settlers west. The U.S. government had treaties (written agreements) with many Indian nations, but the settlers wanted more and more Indian land, and the government broke most of the treaties.

55   On the Great Plains, the buffalo was central to the way of life of almost 200,000 Indians. In 1869, there were 15 million buffalo on the plains. Buffalo meat was important in the Indian diet. Buffalo skin was necessary for clothing, shoes, and housing. Buffalo bones were good for tools and weapons. Also, the buffalo was central to the religion of the Plains Indians. But railroad workers

60 killed thousands of buffalo for meat, and other Americans killed buffalo for "sport" or for their skin. By 1889, there were only a few hundred of the animals left.

    After a long history of wars and broken treaties, most Indians were living on reservations (land from the government) in terrible conditions. Many died of

65 hunger or disease. In the late 1800s, the government began to "Americanize" the Native Americans. The Indians' way of life was never the same again.

Source: *America Is* (Drewry and O'Connor)

AFTER READING

A. CHECK YOUR UNDERSTANDING On a separate piece of paper, write your answers to these questions. When you finish, compare your answers with a partner's answers.

1. Large numbers of people were able to move west after May 10, 1869. Why?

2. Why did many people want to move west? (Give three or more reasons.)

3. How did the railroad change the western part of the United States?

B. VOCABULARY CHECK. Look back at the reading on pages 152–153. Find and highlight words for the definitions below. Write the words next to the correct definitions. Line references are given to help you find the words.

1. the wild area where there were no towns or cities (Lines 2–3): _____

2. the metal and wood path for a train (Lines 16–17): _____

3. towns where nobody lives now (Lines 31–33): _____

4. hard journeys when cowboys led thousands of cattle north (Lines 37–39): _____

5. people who moved west to settle on land and farm it (Lines 40–41): _____

6. huge spaces of flat land in the midwest (Line 43): _____

7. written agreements between nations (Line 52): _____

8. land that Native Americans live on (Lines 63–65): _____

Test-Taking Strategy

Finding Unstated Details

On many standardized tests, some questions ask, "What does the reading passage *not* mention?" or "What is *not* true, according to the reading?" or something similar. In this type of question, there are four possible answers. Find the three that are in the reading passage. The correct answer will be the *other* one—the one that *isn't* in the reading.

C. FINDING DETAILS Look back at the reading to answer these questions. Fill in the correct bubbles.

1. What does the reading *not* mention?

   (A) The new Americans were always moving west.

   (B) They wanted freedom and adventure.

   (C) The trip was hard.

   (D) Native Americans often attacked the people who moved west.

2. The reading does *not* suggest that

   (A) the railroad made a big change in the country.

   (B) Native Americans worked to build the railroad.

   (C) ten miles of track is a lot of work to do in one day.

   (D) people were happy when the railroad was complete.

3. What information is *not* in the reading?

Ⓐ Texas had good land for cattle.

Ⓑ Many people in the north wanted to eat beef.

Ⓒ Cowboys had an exciting life.

Ⓓ There were no cattle drives after 1900.

4. What is *not* true, according to the reading?

Ⓐ Homesteaders went in search of gold.

Ⓑ The Homestead Act was a law from Congress.

Ⓒ Homesteaders farmed land on the plains.

Ⓓ Life wasn't easy for homesteaders.

5. According to the reading, what was *not* a reason that Native Americans hunted buffalo?

Ⓐ meat   Ⓑ sport, for fun   Ⓒ skin for housing   Ⓓ bones for tools

Reading Strategy

Finding Specific Support

Good readers look for specific information that supports general ideas in a reading. Usually, the specific information–one or more details–follows a more general idea. If you can find the specific support, you probably understand the reading.

D. FINDING SPECIFIC SUPPORT Find specific information in the reading on pages 152–153 for each general idea below. Write the information on the lines.

1. General: Two railroad companies raced to build a railroad line.

   Specific: sometimes ten miles of track in just one day

2. General: Building the railroad was hard work.

   Specific: _____

3. General: Life on the plains was difficult.

   Specific: _____

4. General: The buffalo was central to the way of life of the Plains Indians.

   Specific: _____

PART **3** ACADEMIC READING
Changing Patterns of Immigration

BEFORE READING

A. VOCABULARY PREPARATION Read the sentences below. The words in red are from the next reading. Circle the correct part of speech for each word in red. Circle n for *noun* or v for *verb*. Then try to guess the meanings of the words from the context. Write your guesses on the lines.

<u>**Parts of Speech**</u>

1. Between 1840 and 1850, 1.5 million **newcomers**   **n**   **v**
journeyed to the United States.

Guess: _____

Dictionary Definition: _____

2. In Ireland, there was a terrible **famine** because the   **n**   **v**
potato crop had failed. Because potatoes were the
most important part of the Irish diet, thousands of
people died of hunger.

Guess: _____

Dictionary Definition: _____

3. Some Americans began to **resent** the new immigrants.   **n**   **v**
They felt anger toward them because they dressed and
sounded "different" and "foreign."

Guess: _____

Dictionary Definition: _____

4. Later, the resentment of immigrants became more   **n**   **v**
serious. It grew into **hostility**. Some Americans formed
anti-immigration groups, and violence broke out in
some places.

Guess: _____

Dictionary Definition: _____

Now look up the words in red in a dictionary. Write the dictionary definitions on the lines under your guesses.

B. PREVIEWING Scan—look over very quickly—the reading. Write the two headings on the lines. What are the subtopics (specific subjects) of the reading?

_____   _____

C. SCANNING FOR SPECIFIC INFORMATION In the reading, there is information about immigrants from several places. Scan the reading. From which places did people come to the United States in the second half of the 19th century? Write the names of the places on the lines.

_____   _____

_____   _____

_____

D. THINKING AHEAD In small groups, discuss these questions.

1. What are some reasons that people move to a new country?

2. Sometimes, new immigrants become **scapegoats**. In other words, angry people believe these immigrants are responsible for everything bad in society. What are some examples of social problems today? Are any immigrant groups scapegoats?

READING

Read about immigration. As you read, think about the question below. When you find the answer, highlight it.
• What were some differences between the "Old Immigration" and the "New Immigration"?

Changing Patterns of Immigration

The "Old Immigration"

    During the period of "Old Immigration," which started in the 1830s, there was a great wave of immigration to the United States. Between 1840 and 1850, 1.5 million newcomers journeyed to the United States. Nearly half were
5 from Ireland. At that time, there was a terrible famine in Ireland because the potato crop had failed, and the Irish came to find work and to escape starvation. Between 1846 and 1860, 1.5 million Irish came to America. Most settled in New York and Boston. Many others moved west to work on the railroad.

10   In the 1840s, large numbers of Germans also began to come to America. Some left their homeland because of crop failures. Others came to escape political persecution from their governments. Others were German Jews who came for religious freedom. Large numbers of these German immigrants settled

on farms and in cities in the Midwest—areas that were growing fast and had job opportunities.

Chinese immigrants began to come to the Pacific Coast in the 1850s. Many worked in mining towns in the West. Central Pacific Railroad Company hired many more to build the railroad. By the mid-1870s, about 100,000 Chinese were living in California, Oregon, and Washington.

There was something different about this period of immigration from earlier periods. During the colonial years, workers were needed in all of the colonies, so immigrants were welcome. But in the 1840s and 1850s, some native-born Americans began to resent the newcomers (especially the Irish and Germans) and feel anger toward them. Some Americans resented them because they dressed and sounded "different" and because many had "strange" religions like Catholicism or Judaism.

The "New Immigration"

Until the 1880s, most newcomers were from the nations of western Europe. After 1865, many people began to come from southern and eastern Europe—from Italy, Russia, Poland, and the Austro-Hungarian Empire. Most of these newcomers were poor. They hoped to find a better life in America. For many, immigration was the only way to escape persecution in their homeland. One Jewish immigrant noted that "the only hope for the Jews in Russia is to become Jews out of Russia."

These new immigrants moved to the cities. They lived together in neighborhoods such as "Little Italy" or the Jewish Lower East Side in New York City. They spoke their native languages and kept their customs. They built churches, synagogues, clubs, and started newspapers like the ones in their homeland.

These huge waves of immigration caused social problems. The newcomers lived in their own neighborhoods and kept the customs of the "old country." Therefore, many Americans wondered, "Will they ever become part of American life?" Some people, especially workers, believed that the immigrants caused workers' pay

An immigrant neighborhood in New York

to remain low. Some Americans were afraid of the newcomers. They thought these people wanted to destroy the government.

The old resentment of immigrants became more serious. It grew into hostility toward both European and Chinese immigrants. Some Americans formed
60 anti-immigration groups. In some parts of the country, local governments passed laws that took away some immigrants' rights. Violence broke out during the economic depression of 1873: in California, American workers without jobs attacked the Chinese. Then in 1882, Congress passed the Chinese Exclusion Act. This law stopped almost all immigration from China for 10 years.

65 Some historians explain this hostility toward immigrants. There were big changes in American society at that time due to industrialization. Cities began to grow very large very quickly. For native-born Americans who were uncomfortable with these and other changes, the foreign-born people became scapegoats.

Source: *History of a Free Nation* (Bragdon, McCutchen, and Ritchie)

AFTER READING

Critical Thinking Strategy

Using a T-Chart

One type of graphic organizer is a T-chart. It's called a T-chart because it looks like a *t*. To compare two things, write the topics that you are comparing on each side of a T-chart. Then write how the two topics are the same and how they are different.

Example:	**Ben Franklin**	**Phillis Wheatley**
	published books lived in an English colony	published books lived in an English colony
	born in Boston lived in freedom all his life	born in Senegal lived in slavery for many years

A. CHECK YOUR UNDERSTANDING How was the "Old Immigration" different from the "New Immigration"? Look back at the reading to fill in the T-chart.

	Old Immigration	New Immigration
1. When did this period start?	1830s	1865
2. Where did the people come from?		
3. Where did the immigrants settle?		
4. What were the Americans' attitudes toward the newcomers?		

B. PRONOUN REFERENCE Highlight the nouns or noun phrases that the pronouns in red refer to.

1. In the 1840s and 1850s, some native-born Americans began to resent newcomers. **They** felt anger toward them because these people dressed and sounded "different," and many had a "strange" religion.

2. These new immigrants moved to cities in the east. **They** lived together in neighborhoods such as "Little Italy" or the Jewish Lower East Side in New York City.

3. The old resentment of immigrants became more serious. **It** grew into hostility.

Reading Strategy

Understanding Cause and Effect

The words and phrases below indicate cause and effect. *Because, because of,* and *due to* come before a clause or noun that shows **cause**.

***because* + clause**	Some people moved west **because they hoped to find gold.**
***because of* + noun**	Many people moved to America **because of the famine.**
***due to* + noun**	There were big changes **due to industrialization**.

Therefore and *so* mean "That's why." They come before a clause that shows **effect**.

***therefore* + clause**	The immigrants needed money. **Therefore, they worked very hard**.
***so* + clause**	Some people were afraid of the immigrants, **so they formed anti-immigration groups**.

 C. FINDING REASONS Look back at the reading on pages 157–159 to answer the following questions. Look for words such as *because, due to, because of, so,* and *therefore*. The numbers in parentheses refer to lines in the reading.

1. Why was there a famine in Ireland? (Lines 5–6)

_____

2. Why did some Germans come to America? (Lines 10–13)

_____

3. Why were immigrants welcome during the colonial years? (Lines 21–22)

_____

4. Why did some native-born Americans resent the Irish and German newcomers? (Lines 24–26)

_____

5. Why did many Americans wonder, "Will the newcomers ever become part of American life?" (Lines 45–53)

_____

D. MAKING COMPARISONS Look at the details in the pairs of pictures from the 19th century (pages 161–163). Each pair has both similarities and differences. In small groups, use your knowledge from the readings in the chapter to discuss these questions:

• What do you see in each picture? Who are the people? What are they doing? (You might need a dictionary for some vocabulary.)
• How are the two pictures in each pair similar to each other? How are they different from each other?

Now on a separate piece of paper, make a T-chart for each pair of pictures.

a. The Hatch Family

b. A working class family

c. *Wedding of the Rails*

d. *The Song of the Talking Wire*, painting

e. Tom Torlino (Navajo Indian)

f. Tom Torlino in a white school

E. WORD JOURNAL Go back to the readings in Parts 1, 2, and 3. Which words are important for *you* to remember? Put them in your Word Journal.

F. JOURNAL WRITING Choose *one* of these topics:

• something that you learned from these readings
• native people in a country that you know well

• your response to something in these readings
• immigrants in a country that you know well

Write about this topic for 10 minutes. Don't worry about grammar. Don't use a dictionary.

PART ④ THE MECHANICS OF WRITING

In Part 4, you will practice using quotations, transition words, and the simple past. You will need this grammar in Part 5 to write a paragraph comparing two historical pictures.

Transition Words of Contrast

When you write about differences between two things, or contrast them, you need to use transition words of contrast.

Examples: but   however (= but)   in contrast

Notice the punctuation in the examples below. Also, notice that *in contrast* is a little different from *but* or *however*. Use *in contrast* for an opposite situation (good/bad, work/play, etc.).

Examples: There were treaties with the Native Americans**, but** the government broke most of them.

There were treaties with the Native Americans**. However,** the government broke most of them.

Many Americans were able to begin new and exciting lives in the West. **In contrast,** many Native Americans suffered as their way of life changed forever.

A. SENTENCE COMBINING Rewrite each pair of sentences. Combine them with a comma and *but* or begin the second sentence with *However* and a comma or *In contrast* and a comma.

1. The railroad made it possible for many thousands of people to move west. It also made it possible for them to take Native-American land.

_____

_____

2. Many people hoped to get rich in the gold and silver mines. Very few were successful.

_____

_____

3. Mining towns were very busy places for a few years. Most of them are now ghost towns.

_____

_____

4. Some people became rich by mining. Levi Strauss became rich by selling jeans to the miners.

_____

_____

Using *There + Be*

Many sentences begin with *There + be (is, are, was, were)* instead of a subject. In this kind of sentence, the verb *be* agrees with the word(s) that follow it.

Examples: **There was** a need for beef in eastern cities.
There were millions of acres of good grassland.
There wasn't a transcontinental railroad until 1869.

B. USING *THERE + BE* Fill in the blanks with the simple past of the verbs in parentheses. Pay special attention to sentences that begin with *There*.

Urbanization

In the second half of the 19th century, huge numbers of people _____ (come)

to live in U.S. cities, and the cities _____ (grow) fast. Many of these people

_____ (be) from the American countryside, but a large group _____
            3   4

(be) from other countries, mostly European. In many ways, cities at this time _____
                                                                                          5

(be) horrible places. There _____ (be not) enough housing, so people
                                6

_____ (crowd) together in tenements—ugly apartment buildings with small, dark
      7

rooms, many without windows. Garbage _____ (pile) up in the streets, and disease
                                              8

_____ (spread) quickly. People _____ (throw) garbage into rivers,
      9   10

and smoke from thousands of houses and factories _____ (fill) the air. There
                                                          11

_____ (be) almost no public parks or gardens. There _____ (be not)
      12   13

enough firefighters or police.

Most of the poor _____ (work) in factories. These factories _____
                        14   15

(be) dark, dangerous, unhealthy places to work, and there _____ (be) frequent
                                                                  16

injuries. Even young children—some only six years old—_____ (spend) all day at
                                                              17

work in these places. They _____ (not go) to school at all.
                                18

In 1889, in Chicago, Jane Addams _____ (open) Hull House, a settlement house for
                                        19

immigrants and the poor. It _____ (offer) classes in English, hot lunches for factory
                                20

workers, day care for children, a room with art, and a place to exercise. By 1900, there

_____ (be) almost a hundred settlement houses in U.S. cities.
    21

In 1890, a New York newspaper reporter named Jacob A. Riis _____ (write) a book
              22

called *How the Other Half Lives*. It _____ (shock) many middle-class and rich people.
         23

Soon, new laws _____ (begin) to help the poor. Riis also _____
     24   25

(take) a friend of his into the tenements, factories, and jails to show him the worst problems and

"educate" him. This friend, Theodore Roosevelt, later _____ (become) president of
         26

the United States.

Source: *History of a Free Nation* (Bragdon, McCutchen, and Ritchie)

Using Quotations to Support General Statements

When you write a paragraph, you need to give specific information to support (explain, prove) your general statements. One kind of specific support is a short quotation of someone's exact words.

Example: Life was difficult for miners in the west. (**general statement**) As a miner in Montana put it, "We came looking for gold and easy times, but we found only mud and hardship." (**specific support**)

Quotations support your general ideas. They can also make your writing more interesting and colorful. Be sure to do the following when you use a quotation:

1. Give credit to your source. In other words, who said this?
2. Use quotation marks.
3. Don't change any words.

Here are some ways to introduce a quotation:

As Liana Alvarez said, "..."

According to Tom Brainard, a homesteader in Oklahoma, "..."

As one homesteader put it, "..."

One homesteader noted, "..."

C. USING QUOTATIONS Read the following quotations. Then use the quotations to support the statements below.

I've never seen so many insects, so little rain, so much trouble and death in my life.
—a farmer in Kansas, 1851

We worked in snow and heat, mountains and desert, sometimes 15 hours a day. We built every inch of that track by hand. —"Johnny" Wu, railroad worker, 1867

In America we wouldn't be under someone's boot. We would work hard but get a fair wage, enough food, and maybe have a good life someday. —Brigit O'Connor, immigrant from Ireland, 1886

There was a lot of dust and dirt, hard work and worry, and never enough sleep. Mostly it was damn boring. —Lester Mullin, cowboy, 1891

They killed my family, my tribe. They took our land and left us nothing.
—Lame Horse, Sioux Indian, 1855

1. We think of cowboys as romantic figures who had exciting lives. However, most of the time the life of a cowboy was not only difficult but also very far from exciting.

   _____

   _____

2. Homesteaders led hard lives, quite different from the lives of their friends and relatives back home in small eastern towns.

   _____

   _____

3. Many whites treated the Sioux as less than human.

   _____

   _____

4. The building of the transcontinental railroad required backbreaking labor by thousands of workers, mostly immigrants.

   _____

   _____

5. Life in the new country wasn't easy, but it was better than the life that most people had left behind. It gave them hope.

   _____

   _____

D. REVIEW/EDITING There are at least seven mistakes in the paragraph. They are mistakes with the punctuation of transition words, the use of *there*, the simple past, and the use of quotations. Find and correct them.

These pictures of two families show a contrast in the way people lived in nineteenth-century America. Both families ~~was~~ *were* large but the similarity ends there. One picture tells us that some people was wealthy and lived in great comfort. This family lived in a large house with art, expensive carpets, and long drapes that covered high windows. Their clothing was beautiful and clean. The children had toys to play with. Apparently, education was important; several family members are reading in this picture. In contrast the other picture tells us that some people were very poor. This family live in a small, dark apartment with laundry hanging on the stove to dry. Their clothing was shabby and not very clean. There isn't any toys or books in the photo. The life of these working-class people was probably very difficult, especially in a country of such wealth. To be a poor man is hard, but to be a poor race in a land of dollars is the very bottom of hardships.

PART ⑤ ACADEMIC WRITING

WRITING ASSIGNMENT

In Part 5, you will write a paragraph about one of the pairs of pictures on pages 162–163. In your paragraph, answer this question: What do these pictures tell us about American life in the second half of the 19th century?

Use both the pictures and your knowledge of U.S. history from the readings in Parts 2 and 3 of this chapter. Begin your paragraph with one of these topic sentences:

- These two pictures show us how differently people thought about the end of the frontier.
- These two photos give us an example of how life changed for American Indians in the late 19th century.

Somewhere in your paragraph, include one quotation from Part 1 (pages 147–148) to support one of your general statements. Your quotation should be short—just one or two sentences.

STEP A. CHOOSING A TOPIC It's important to choose a topic that you understand and have ideas about. Choose *one* pair of photos from page 162–163.

STEP B. PLANNING YOUR PARAGRAPH Follow these steps:

1. Find the T-chart that you created for this pair of pictures (Activity D, page 161).
2. Add as many details as you can.
3. For new words, use a dictionary or ask someone—another student or your teacher.
4. Which quotation did you choose for this pair of pictures? If the quotation is long, choose just one good sentence from it.

Writing Strategy ⬤⬤⬤

Writing a Paragraph of Comparison

In a paragraph of comparison, you write about the similarities and differences between two people, things, places, or ideas. (In the case of this chapter, you'll write about the ideas behind two pictures.) One way to do this is to begin with your main idea in a topic sentence and then list the similarities and next the differences. When you write about the differences, discuss one picture first and then the other. It's important to give specific support after each general statement.

Example:

   These pictures of two families show an enormous contrast in the way people lived in nineteenth-century America. (Topic sentence) Both families were very large, but the similarity ends there. One picture tells us that some people were extremely wealthy and lived in great comfort. (General statement) This family lived in a large house with art, expensive carpets, and long drapes that covered high windows. Their clothing was beautiful and clean. The children had toys to play with. Apparently, education was important; several family members are reading in this picture. (Specific support) In contrast, the other picture tells us that some people were very poor. (General statement) This family lived in a small, dark apartment with laundry hanging on the stove to dry. Their clothing was shabby, ill-fitting, and not very clean. There don't appear to be any toys or books in the photo. The life of these working-class people was probably very difficult, especially in a country of such wealth. (Specific support) As W. E. B. Du Bois pointed out, "To be a poor man is hard, but to be a poor race in land of dollars is the very bottom of hardships." (Concluding quotation)

Notice in the example:

• the general statement about the first picture
• the supporting details for this general statement
• the general statement about the second picture
• the supporting details about this general statement
• the use of tenses
• the use of one short quotation
• the use of transition expressions for contrast

STEP C. WRITING THE PARAGRAPH Use your notes from Step B. Write complete sentences in paragraph form. You might make some mistakes, but don't worry about them at this point.

STEP D. EDITING Read your paragraph and answer these questions.

1. Is the paragraph form correct (indentation, margins)?

2. Is there a general statement about each picture?

3. Are there specific details to support each general statement?

4. Is there a transition expression of contrast to move from one picture to the other?

5. Is the simple past tense used correctly?

6. Do the transition words of contrast have correct punctuation?

7. Are the punctuation and credit (the source) correct for the quotation?

STEP E. REWRITING Write your paragraph again, without the mistakes.

UNIT ③ VOCABULARY WORKSHOP

Review vocabulary that you learned in Chapters 5 and 6.

A. MATCHING Match the definitions to the words. Write the correct letters on the lines.

_____ **1.** autobiography

_____ **2.** droughts

_____ **3.** famine

_____ **4.** journey

_____ **5.** railroad

_____ **6.** retire

_____ **7.** settlers

_____ **8.** slave

_____ **9.** theory

_____ **10.** treaties

a. long periods with no rain

b. stop working

c. written agreements

d. idea

e. long trip

f. trains

g. person who is owned by another

h. book about a person's own life

i. situation when many people die because there isn't enough food

j. people who move to a new place to live there permanently

B. TRUE OR FALSE? Which sentences are true? Which are false? Fill in Ⓣ for *True* or Ⓕ for *False*.

1. A **miner** digs gold from the ground.   Ⓣ   Ⓕ

2. Angry, unhappy people might have **grievances**.   Ⓣ   Ⓕ

3. A **pamphlet** is a long book.   Ⓣ   Ⓕ

4. There are a lot of trees on the **plains**.   Ⓣ   Ⓕ

5. Children sometimes fly **kites** on a windy day.   Ⓣ   Ⓕ

6. Beef, chicken, and lamb are examples of **crops**.   Ⓣ   Ⓕ

7. The **frontier** is far from cities and most towns.   Ⓣ   Ⓕ

8. People give **scapegoats** the credit for doing something good.   Ⓣ   Ⓕ

C. WORDS IN PHRASES Write the words and phrases from the box on the lines below to complete the phrases.

a law	beliefs	business	drive	house	their religion	town

1. the printing _____

2. practiced _____

3. religious _____

4. a ghost _____

5. a log _____

6. a cattle _____

7. passed _____

D. HIGH FREQUENCY WORDS Some of the most common words in English are in the box below. They are among the most frequent 500-1000 words. Fill in the blanks with words from this box. When you finish, check your answers in the reading on pages 126–127.

born	colonial	first	popular	thirteen
both	exceptions	history	taught	unusual

Not many women were well-known during _____colonial_____ times. And almost no
                                          1

women became published poets. However, there were some _____. Unlike
                                                              2

most slave women, Phillis Wheatley received an education. She also became a

_____ poet in _____ England and America.
        3   4

Phillis Wheatley was _____ in Senegal, Africa about 1753. In 1761, John
                              5

and Susannah Wheatley bought her as a slave in Boston. The Wheatleys _____ her
                                                                              6

to read and write. This was _____: most slave owners did not want to educate
                                    7

their slaves. Phillis also learned _____, geography, and Latin.
                                          8

Phillis wrote her _____ poem at the age of _____.
                          9   10

APPENDIX 1 SPELLING RULES

Rules for adding an -s for the plural form and the third person singular of verbs in the simple present tense:

1. Add -es to words that end in -ch, -s, -sh, -x, or -z.

   catch   →   catches
   kiss   →   kisses
   push   →   pushes
   fix   →   fixes
   buzz   →   buzzes

2. If the simple form of a verb ends in a consonant + y, change the y to i and add -es.

   fly   →   flies
   study   →   studies

   Note: Do not change the y or add an e if the simple form ends in vowel + y.

   enjoy   →   enjoys
   stay   →   stays

3. For most other verbs, just add -s.

   think   →   thinks
   put   →   puts

Rules for adding -ing:

1. If the simple form of the verb ends in a silent -e, drop the -e and add -ing.

   move   →   moving
   write   →   writing

2. If the simple form ends in -ie, drop the -ie, add y and the -ing.

   die   →   dying
   lie   →   lying

3. If the last three letters are consonant/vowel/consonant in a one-syllable word, double the last consonant and then add -ing.

   put   →   putting
   run   →   running
   drop   →   dropping

   Note: Do not double w, x, or y.

4. For a two-syllable word that ends in consonant/vowel/consonant, there are two rules:

   a. If the accent is on the second syllable, double the final consonant.

      permit   →   permitting

   b. If the accent is on the first syllable, do not double the final consonant.

      happen   →   happening

5. For all other verbs, simply add -ing. Do not drop, add, or change anything.

   work   →   working
   study   →   studying

Rules for adding *-ed* for the past tense or past participle of regular verbs:

1. If the verb already ends in *-e,* just add *-d.*

   move   ➡   moved

   tie   ➡   tied

2. If the verb ends in consonant + *y,* change the *y* to *-ied.*

   hurry   ➡   hurried

   study   ➡   studied

   Note: Do not change the *y* to *-ied* if the verb ends in vowel + *y.*

   enjoy   ➡   enjoyed

   stay   ➡   stayed

3. If the last three letters are consonant/ vowel/consonant in a one-syllable word, double the last consonant and then add *-ed.*

   rub   ➡   rubbed

   stop   ➡   stopped

   Note: Do not double *w, x,* or *y.*

4. For a two-syllable word that ends in consonant/vowel/consonant, there are two rules:

   a. If the accent is on the second syllable, double the final consonant.

   permit   ➡   permitted

   b. If the accent is on the first syllable, do not double the final consonant.

   happen   ➡   happened

5. For all other regular verbs, simply add *-ed.*

   learn   ➡   learned

   want   ➡   wanted

APPENDIX 2 COMMON IRREGULAR VERBS

Simple Present	Simple Past	Past Participle	Simple Present	Simple Past	Past Participle
am/is/are	was/were	been	mean	meant	meant
beat	beat	beat	meet	met	met
become	became	become	pay	paid	paid
begin	began	begun	put	put	put
break	broke	broken	read	read	read
bring	brought	brought	ride	rode	ridden
buy	bought	bought	ring	rang	rung
catch	caught	caught	rise	rose	risen
choose	chose	chosen	run	ran	run
come	come	come	say	said	said
cost	cost	cost	see	saw	seen
cut	cut	cut	send	sent	sent
do	done	done	set	set	set
draw	drew	drawn	shake	shook	shaken
drink	drank	drunk	show	showed	shown
drive	drove	driven	shut	shut	shut
eat	ate	eaten	sing	sang	sung
hear	heard	heard	sink	sank	sunk
fall	fell	fallen	sit	sat	sat
feed	fed	fed	sleep	slept	slept
feel	felt	felt	speak	spoke	spoken
find	found	found	spend	spent	spent
fly	flew	flown	stand	stood	stood
forget	forgot	forgotten	steal	stole	stolen
freeze	froze	frozen	stick	stuck	stuck
get	got	gotten/got	sweep	swept	swept
give	gave	given	swim	swam	swum
go	went	gone	take	took	taken
grow	grew	grown	teach	taught	taught
hit	hit	hit	tear	tore	torn
hold	held	held	tell	told	told
keep	kept	kept	think	thought	thought
know	knew	known	throw	threw	thrown
lay	laid	laid	wake	woke	woken
leave	left	left	wear	wore	worn
lend	lent	lent	win	won	won
lose	lost	lost	wind	wound	wound
make	made	made	write	wrote	written

Stative (Nonaction) Verbs

Certain verbs don't use the present continuous tense, even if the action is "right now." Instead, use the simple present tense with these stative (nonaction) verbs.

Condition	Possession	Emotional or Mental Activity		
consist	belong	appreciate	know	remember
cost	contain	approve	like	understand
equal	own	believe	love	want
matter	possess	desire	mean	
owe		dislike	need	
resemble	Perception	doubt	prefer	
	seem	hate	recognize	

Verbs with Stative and Nonstative Meanings

Some verbs have more than one meaning. In the stative (nonaction) meaning, the verb is in the simple present tense. In the nonstative (action) meaning, the verb is in the present continuous if the action is happening right now. Here are some of these verbs with their meanings.

Verbs	Stative Meaning	Nonstative Meaning
Condition:		
be	He is tall.	He's being very good. (be = behave/act)
fit	The suit fits well.	The tailor is fitting him for a new suit. (fit = measure for; cause to fit or conform)
match	Her shoes match her dress. (match = looks attractive with)	I'm matching this tie with these shirts. (match = try to put together)
weigh	He weighs 150 pounds.	He's weighing himself now. (weigh = put on a scale)
Possession:		
have	I have a new car. (have = possess)	I'm having some problems. (have = experience) He's having breakfast. (have = eat/drink) She's having a baby. (have = be pregnant with or give birth to) They're having a party. (have = give)

Verbs	Stative Meaning	Nonstative Meaning
Perception:		

appear	He appears to be ready.
	   (appear = seem)
		She's appearing in a new play.
		   (appear = perform or come into sight)

feel	I feel it's a good idea.
	   (feel = think/believe)
	 He feels relieved.
	   (feel = have an emotion)
		I'm feeling better now. (feel = experience
		   an emotion or physical feeling)
		 She's feeling around for the light switch.
		   (feel = touch)

hear	He doesn't hear you.
	   (hear = perceive with the ears)
		You'll be hearing from my lawyer.
		   (hear = get a letter or call)

look	You look tired.
	
	   (look = seem)
		He's looking at you.
		
		   (look = use one's eyes)

see	I see him over there.
	   (see = perceive with the eyes)
		The mayor is seeing her now.
		   (see = meet with)

smell	This smells good!
	   (smell = have a smell)
		She's smelling every perfume in the store.
		   (smell = sniff)

sound	That sounds like a good idea.
	   (sound = seem)
	 The music sounds loud.
	   (sound = have a sound)
		They're sounding the alarm.
		   (sound = cause a sound)

taste	This tastes great!
	   (taste = have a taste)
	 I taste something strange.
	   (taste = perceive a taste)
		He's tasting your cake now.
		   (taste = try, sample food)

Emotional/Mental Activity:		

guess	I guess we should start.
	   (guess = suppose)
		He's just guessing.
		   (guess = make an estimate)

imagine	I imagine that you're tired.
	   (imagine = guess, think)
		You're just imagining things.
		   (imagine = use the imagination)

mean	It means "no."
	   (mean = signify)
		I've been meaning to do that.
		   (mean = intend)

mind	I don't mind.
	   (mind = object to
		Who's minding the store?
		   (mind = take care of)
		 The boy is minding his mother.
		   (mind = do what is asked)

think	I think it's too big.
	   (think = believe, have an opinion)
		Wait a second, I'm thinking.
		   (think = consider, reflect)

Below are the most common words on the Academic Word List. This list is put together at the School of Linguistics and Applied Language Studies at Victoria University of Wellington, New Zealand.

Each word in italics is the most frequently occurring member of the word family in the Academic Corpus. For example, *analysis* is the most common form of the word family <u>analyse</u>.

analyse
  analysed
  analyser
  analysers
  analyses
  analysing
  analysis
  analyst
  analysts
  analytic
  analytical
  analytically
  analyze
  analyzed
  analyzes
  analyzing
approach
  approachable
  approached
  approaches
  approaching
  unapproachable
area
  areas
assess
  assessable

  assessed
  assesses
  assessing
  assessment
  assessments
  reassess
  reassessed
  reassessing
  reassessment
  unassessed
assume
  assumed
  assumes
  assuming
  assumption
  assumptions
authority
  authoritative
  authorities
available
  availability
  unavailable
benefit
  beneficial
  beneficiary
  beneficiaries

  benefited
  benefiting
  benefits
concept
  conception
  concepts
  conceptual
  conceptualisation
  conceptualise
  conceptualised
  conceptualises
  conceptualising
  conceptually
consist
  consisted
  consistency
  consistent
  consistently
  consisting
  consists
  inconsistencies
  inconsistency
  inconsistent
constitute
  constituencies
  constituency

constituent
constituents
constituted
constitutes
constituting
constitution
constitutions
constitutional
constitutionally
constitutive
unconstitutional
context
contexts
contextual
contextualise
contextualised
contextualising
uncontextualised
contextualize
contextualized
contextualizing
uncontextualized
contract
contracted
contracting
contractor
contractors
contracts
create
created
creates
creating
creation
creations
creative
creatively
creativity

creator
creators
recreate
recreated
recreates
recreating
data
define
definable
defined
defines
defining
definition
definitions
redefine
redefined
redefines
redefining
undefined
derive
derivation
derivations
derivative
derivatives
derived
derives
deriving
distribute
distributed
distributing
distribution
distributional
distributions
distributive
distributor
distributors
redistribute

redistributed
redistributes
redistributing
redistribution
economy
economic
economical
economically
economics
economies
economist
economists
uneconomical
environment
environmental
environmentalist
environmentalists
environmentally
environments
establish
disestablish
disestablished
disestablishes
disestablishing
disestablishment
established
establishes
establishing
establishment
establishments
estimate
estimated
estimates
estimating
estimation
estimations
over-estimate

overestimate
overestimated
overestimates
overestimating
underestimate
underestimated
underestimates
underestimating
evident
   evidenced
   evidence
   evidential
   evidently
export
   exported
   exporter
   exporters
   exporting
   exports
factor
   factored
   factoring
   factors
finance
   financed
   finances
   financial
   financially
   financier
   financiers
   financing
formula
   formulae
   formulas
   formulate
   formulated
   formulating

formulation
formulations
reformulate
reformulated
reformulating
reformulation
reformulations
function
   functional
   functionally
   functioned
   functioning
   functions
identify
   identifiable
   identification
   identified
   identifies
   identifying
   identities
   identity
   unidentifiable
income
   incomes
indicate
   indicated
   indicates
   indicating
   indication
   indications
   indicative
   indicator
   indicators
individual
   individualised
   individuality
   individualism

individualist
individualists
individualistic
individually
individuals
interpret
   interpretation
   interpretations
   interpretative
   interpreted
   interpreting
   interpretive
   interprets
   misinterpret
   misinterpretation
   misinterpretations
   misinterpreted
   misinterpreting
   misinterprets
   reinterpret
   reinterpreted
   reinterprets
   reinterpreting
   reinterpretation
   reinterpretations
involve
   involved
   involvement
   involves
   involving
   uninvolved
issue
   issued
   issues
   issuing
labour
   labor

labored
labors
laboured
labouring
labours
legal
   illegal
   illegality
   illegally
   legality
   legally
legislate
   legislated
   legislates
   legislating
   legislation
   legislative
   legislator
   legislators
   legislature
major
   majorities
   majority
method
   methodical
   methodological
   methodologies
   methodology
   methods
occur
   occurred
   occurrence
   occurrences
   occurring
   occurs
   reoccur
   reoccurred

reoccurring
reoccurs
percent
   percentage
   percentages
period
   periodic
   periodical
   periodically
   periodicals
   periods
policy
   policies
principle
   principled
   principles
   unprincipled
proceed
   procedural
   procedure
   procedures
   proceeded
   proceeding
   proceedings
   proceeds
process
   processed
   processes
   processing
require
   required
   requirement
   requirements
   requires
   requiring
research
   researched

researcher
researchers
researches
researching
respond
   responded
   respondent
   respondents
   responding
   responds
   response
   responses
   responsive
   responsiveness
   unresponsive
role
   roles
section
   sectioned
   sectioning
   sections
sector
   sectors
significant
   insignificant
   insignificantly
   significance
   significantly
   signified
   signifies
   signify
   signifying
similar
   dissimilar
   similarities
   similarity
   similarly

source
- sourced
- sources
- sourcing

specific
- specifically
- specification
- specifications
- specificity
- specifics

structure
- restructure
- restructured
- restructures
- restructuring

structural
structurally
structured
structures
structuring
unstructured

theory
- theoretical
- theoretically
- theories
- theorist
- theorists

vary
- invariable
- invariably

variability
variable
variables
variably
variance
variant
variants
variation
variations
varied
varies
varying

VOCABULARY INDEX

● ● ● ● ● SKILLS INDEX

Eating insects, 97, 100
Expansion activities, 46, 72, 81, 100
Free enterprise system, 49
Insects (eating), 97, 100
Jobs, 28, 31, 36
Majors, 31
Nutrition, 108
Preparation activities, 52, 73, 97, 130, 151, 156
Prepositions, 37, 56
Revolution (American, Road to), 130, 135
Suffixes, 7
for professions (*-or, -er. –ist,* or *–ian*), 36
Unusual animals, 72
Workshops,
    Biology (Unit 2), 115-116
    Business (Unit 1), 65-66
    U.S. History (Unit 3), 171-172

WRITING

Journals, SEE Journals (separate heading)

Strategies

Choosing a topic, 11, 41, 64, 90, 113, 142, 169
Determining the main idea, 42
Editing your paragraph, 14, 42, 64, 91, 114, 143, 170
Organizing paragraphs,
    of analysis, 114
    of comparison, 169
    of description, 64
    of process, 91
Planning your paragraph, 12, 42, 64, 90, 113, 143, 169
Rewriting paragraph, 42, 64, 91, 114, 143, 170
Writing a paragraph, 13-14, 42, 64, 91, 114, 143, 170
Writing a summary, 142

Writing Skills (Mechanics of Writing)
Condensing, 140-141
Editing, 89, 141, 168
Grammar,
    a, 89
    a lot of, 111
    an, 89
    adjectives, 62-63
        multiple adjectives, 62-63
    and, 87
    articles (*a/an/the*), 89
    because, 87
    but, 164
    can, 137
        causatives (*force, make*), 138
        could, 137
    count nouns, 109-110
    direct objects, 88
        force, 138
        gerunds (and infinitives), 41
        however, 164
        if (not) . . . will, 111
        in contrast, 164
    indirect objects, 88
    infinitives (and gerunds), 41
    irregular verbs, 175 (Appendix 2)
    make, 138
    noncount nouns, 109-110
    nonstative verbs, 176-177 (Appendix 3)
    not enough, 111
    nouns (count/noncount, food), 109-110
    objects (direct/ indirect), 88
    past tense, 86, 137
    prepositions,
    of place, 58-60
    present perfect, 39, 40
    time expressions with, 39
    simple past, 39-40, 86, 137
    simple present, 38, 40

stative verbs, 61-62, 176-177 (Appendix 3)
    adjectives with, 62
    multiple adjectives with, 62
    the, 89
    there + be, 165-166
    time phrases, 87
    too many, 110
    too much, 110
    transition words of contrast, 164
    when, 87
    words in phrases (prepositions), 37, 56
Quotations (to support general statements), 166-167
Spelling,
    irregular verbs, 175 (Appendix 2)
    past participles, 174 (Appendix 1)
    past tense, 174 (Appendix 1)
    simple present, 38
Summary writing, 140-141

Writing Topics
19th century America, 169
Advertisements, 64
America,
    19th century, 169
    Colonial, 142
Books, 11-14
Colonial America (summarizing), 142
Diet, 113-114
Ideal job, 41-42
Self-description, 40

CREDITS

Text Credits

p. 27 Adapted from *100 Great Jobs and How to Get Them*, by Richard Fein, 1999. Impact Publishing. Also adapted from Career Services Website - www.cofc.edu/~career. P. 48 Adapted from *Introduction to Business: Our Business and Economic World,* 1995 by Glencoe/McGraw-Hill. Reprinted with permission of the McGraw-Hill Companies. p. 53 Adapted from *Scholastic Update, Teachers Edition*, May 7, 1993. Copyright © 1993 by Scholastic Inc. Reprinted by permission. p. 54 Excerpts from "Hot Markets for 2004" by Chris Penttila and Nicole L. Torres. Reprinted with permission from *Entrepreneur Magazine*, November 21, 2003, www.entrepreneur.com. p. 71 Adapted from *Best Friends Magazine*, May/June 2004. p. 74 Adapted from *Biology: The Dynamics of Life*, by Alton Biggs by Whitney Crispen Hagins, Chris Kapicka, Linda Lundgren, Peter Rillero, Kathleen G. Tallman, Dinah Zike, 2004. Reprinted by permission from the McGraw-Hill Companies and the National Geographic Society. p. 79 Adapted from *Biology: The Dynamics of Life*, by Alton Biggs by Whitney Crispen Hagins, Chris Kapicka, Linda Lundgren, Peter Rillero, Kathleen G. Tallman, Dinah Zike, 2004. Reprinted by permission from the McGraw-Hill Companies and the National Geographic Society. p. 95 Adapted from "Globalization," by Erla Zwingle—(Section III) National Geographic Xpeditions—NationalGeographic.com © 2004 National Geographic Society. p 98 Adapted from "For Most People, Eating Bugs Is Only Natural" by Sharon Guynup and Nicolas Ruggia. *National Geographic Channel*, July 15, 2004. p 103 Adapted from *Biology: An Everyday Experience* by Albert Kaskel, Paul J. Hummer, and Lucy Daniel, 1999, 1995, 1992 by Glencoe/McGraw-Hill. Copyright © 1988, 1985, 1981 by Merrill Publishing Company. Reprinted with the permission of the McGraw-Hill Companies. p 121 Adapted from *America Is*, Fifth Edition by Henry N. Drewry and Thomas H. O'Connor, 1995. Glencoe/McGraw-Hill. Reprinted with permission of the McGraw-Hill Companies. p. 125 Adapted from *America Is*, Fifth Edition, by Henry N. Drewry and Thomas H. O'Connor. Copyright © 1995 by Glencoe Publishing Company. Copyright © 1979, 1982, 1984, 1987 by Merrill Publishing Company. Reprinted with the permission of the McGraw-Hill Companies. p. 132 Adapted from *America Is*, Fifth Edition, by Henry N. Drewry and Thomas H. O'Connor. Copyright © 1995 by Glencoe Publishing Company. Copyright © 1979, 1982, 1984, 1987 by Merrill Publishing Company. Reprinted with the permission of the McGraw-Hill Companies. p. 152 Adapted from *America Is*, Fifth Edition, by Henry N. Drewry and Thomas H. O'Connor. Copyright © 1995 by Glencoe Publishing Company. Copyright © 1979, 1982, 1984, 1987 by Merrill Publishing Company. Reprinted with the permission of the McGraw-Hill Companies. p. 157 Adapted from *History of a Free Nation* by Henry W. Bragdon, Samuel P. McCutchen, and Donald A. Ritchie, 1994. Copyright by Glencoe Publishing Company. Reprinted with the permission of the McGraw-Hill Companies. p. 165 Adapted from *History of a Free Nation* by Henry W. Bragdon, Samuel P. McCutchen, and Donald A. Ritchie, 1994. Copyright by Glencoe Publishing Company. Reprinted with the permission of the McGraw-Hill Companies.

Photos Credits

Cover: top right: © PhotoDisc/Getty Images; middle left: © Digital Vision/Getty Images; bottom right: Miramax/Everett Collection.

Getting Started. Opener: © Bananastock/PictureQuest; p. 2: © David Young-Wolff/PhotoEdit; p. 11: © Antonio Mo/Getty Images.

Unit 1. Opener: © Brand X Pictures/PictureQuest; p. 19: © Mark Mainz/Getty Images; p. 20 (top left & top right): © PhotoDisc/Getty Images; p. 20 (bottom let): © Mathew McKee; Eye Uniquitous/CORBIS; p. 20 (bottom right): The McGraw-Hill Companies, Inc./Jill Braaten, Photographer; p. 21: © Stephen O. Muskie/www.outtakes.com; p. 22 (top): Courtesy of Bruce Shelley; p. 22 (bottom): © Stephen O. Muskie/ www.outtakes.com; p. 27: The McGraw-Hill Companies, Inc./Jill Braaten, Photographer; p. 32: © Creastas/PictureQuest; p. 34: © John M. Daugherty/Photo Researchers; p. 35 (right): TRB foto/Getty Images; (middle): Linda S. O'Roke; (left): Creastats/PictureQuest; p. 43: © Reuters/CORBIS; p. 44 (top left): © Jacobs Stock Photography/ Getty Images; p. 44 (middle right): © Michael Newman/PhotoEdit; p. 44 (bottom left): © Mehmet Biber/Photo Researchers; p. 45 (top): © David Madison/Getty Images; p. 45 (bottom): © Evan Agostini/Getty Images; p. 47: © Comstock Images/PictureQuest; p. 50: © PhotoDisc/Getty Images; p. 51: General Motors Media Archive; p. 54 (top and middle): © PhotoDisc/Getty Images; p. 54 (bottom): © Comstock Images/PictureQuest; p. 56 (both): Image courtesy of The Advertising Archives; p. 59 (top): © PhotoDisc/ Getty Images; p. 59 (bottom): Image courtesy of The Advertising Archives.

Unit 2. Opener: © Digital Vision; p. 69: © Creatas Images/PictureQuest; p. 70 (top left): © Creatas Images/PunchStock; p. 70 (top rght): © Clyde H. Smith/Peter Arnold; p. 70 (bottom left): © C & M Denis-Huot/Peter Arnold; p. 70 (bottom right): © Donna and Gilbert Grosvenor/National Geographic Image Collection/Getty Images; p. 71 (top): © Royalty-Free/ CORBIS; p. 71 (bottom): © Barbara Walton/EPA; p. 73 (left): © PhotoDisc/Getty Images; p. 73 (right): © David M. Dennis; p. 75 (left): © Digital Vision/PunchStock; p. 75 (right): © Ron Cohn, The Gorilla Foundation/koko.org; p. 76: © Lawrence Migdale/Photo Researchers; p. 79 (top): © Joel Sartore/National Geographic Image Collection; p. 79 (bottom): © Jacana/Photo Researchers; p. 84 (left): © TimeLife Pictures/Getty Images; p. 84 (right): © SuperStock, Inc./SuperStock; p. 93: © MedioImages/PictureQuest; p. 94 (left): © PhotoDisc/Getty Images; p. 94 (right): © Brian Hagiwara/FoodPix/Getty Images; p. 95: © AFP/Douglas E. Curran/Getty Images; p. 98: © Royalty-Free/CORBIS; p. 99 (top right): © Ken Lucas/Getty Images; p. 99 (bottom left); © Luis Castaneda Inc/Getty Images; p. 103: Royalty-Free/CORBIS; p. 104: Digital Vision/Getty Images.

Unit 3. Opener: © The Granger Collection, New York; p. 119: © Rob Crandall/The Image Works; p. 120 (all), 121 (all), 122 (all), 124 (top): © The Granger Collection, New York; p. 124 (bottom): A Plantation, Slave Quarters. The Maryland Historical Society, Baltimore, Maryland; p. 125: © Bettmann/CORBIS; p. 126: © Museum of the City of New York/CORBIS; p. 127: © CORBIS; p. 132, 133: © The Granger Collection, New York; p. 145: © Miramax/Everett Collection; p. 146 (top): © The Granger Collection, New York; p. 146 (bottom left): © Archive Holdings Inc/Getty Images; p. 146 (bottom right): © Bettmann/CORBIS; p. 147 (top): © Photo Collection Alexander Alland, Sr./CORBIS; p. 147 (bottom): © Bettmann/CORBIS; p. 150 (top): © The Granger Collection, New York; p. 150 (middle and bottom): © CORBIS; p. 152: © The Granger Collection, New York; p. 158: © CORBIS; p. 162 (top): © The Granger Collection, New York; p. 162 (middle): © Bettmann/CORBIS; p. 162 (bottom): AP/Wide World Photos; p. 163 (top): The Song of the Talking Wire, Henry F. Family, oil on canvas, 1904 Bequest of Charles Phelps and Anna Sinton Taft, The Taft Museum, Cincinnatic, Ohio; p. 163 (bottom left): Photographic Lot 81-12 06807600, Smithsonian Institution National Anthropological Archives; p. 163 (bottom right): Photographic Lot 81-12 06807100, Smithsonian Institution National Anthropological Archives.

NOTES